Healing Relationships

A CHRISTIAN'S MANUAL FOR LAY COUNSELING

Stephen A. Grunlan
& Daniel H. Lambrides

CHRISTIAN PUBLICATIONS, INC.

Camp Hill, Pennsylvania

Christian Publications, Inc.

Publishing House of

The Christian and Missionary Alliance

3825 Hartzdale Drive

Camp Hill, PA 17011

✝ *The mark of vibrant faith*

Library of Congress Catalog Card Number: 83-70103
ISBN: 0-87509-329-9
Unless otherwise indicated, all quotations are taken from
the HOLY BIBLE: NEW INTERNATIONAL VERSION
and used by permission of Zondervan Bible Publishers
Printed in United States of America

To our wives

Sandy, my wife and best friend,
who has given me love and encouragement
and made our marriage a healing relationship.

Jane, who has helped me learn
to see, and to feel, and in our marriage
has taught me the power of healing relationships.

Healing Relationships

CONTENTS

PREFACE

This is a book about people helping people. More specifically, it is written to help Christian people, motivated by their relationship with the Lord, to minister to others who hurt. Because this book focuses on helping people who hurt, it is a book about healing.

From the beginning, our Lord taught that our relationship with Him should affect our relationships with others, *You are to love one another as I have loved you* (John 13:34-35). The apostle Paul also instructs us, *Be kind to one another, tender-hearted, forgiving one another just as God, for Christ's sake has forgiven you* (Eph. 4:32). Therefore this book is also about relationships.

We have written a book about healing relationships because we believe all Christians are called to minister to each other. In fact, most Christians are ministering to others on a personal basis. The question is not so much should believers counsel each other, because they will. The question is, will they do so effectively?

Originally this book was entitled *Effective Lay Counseling*. We believe that Christians can effectively minister to each other through their interpersonal relationships. With some training, Christians can turn their interpersonal relationships into healing relationships.

We have written this book as a manual for training lay counselors. We believe that Sunday school teachers, youth workers, elders—in fact all members of the church should have some training in counseling skills.

We do not view this book as a complete training program in lay counseling, but rather as a first step in developing the needed skills and techniques. It is our prayer that this book will aid you in the process of developing healing relationships.

Some of you will find that your personal characteristics lend themselves to counseling and you may want to have a broader counseling ministry. In that case you will want to develop further the skills discussed in this manual. Whether or not you decide to become more actively involved in counseling, we hope the concepts and skills presented in this manual will enrich your Christian life and walk.

A book is always more than the product of the authors. Many persons contribute to an effort such as this. We would like to thank Dr. Melvin Kimble of Northwestern Lutheran Theological Seminary and Dr. Vernon Olson and Mr. Tom Morscheck of St. Paul Bible College for their suggestions and support in this project. Dr. Dwenda Gjerdingen and Dr. Richard Warhol read selected sections on medical aspects and as physicians made helpful suggestions. We are grateful for their help. We would also like to thank Frank and Joann DeMarco and David and Sue Jellison for their insights and critique of an early draft of the book. Finally, we would like to thank Carol Anderson for her assistance with the typing of the manuscript. Her help was invaluable.

CHAPTER ONE

Counseling as a Lay Ministry

Jennifer, an attractive fifteen-year-old high school soph-omore, seemed quite distracted during Sunday school class. Mrs. Swanson, her Sunday school teacher, realized that something was bothering Jennifer. When class ended most of the girls dashed out of the room but Jennifer just remained in her seat. Mrs. Swanson went over and sat next to her. She asked Jennifer if everything was okay. Suddenly tears began to roll down her cheeks. Sobbing, she turned to Mrs. Swanson and blurted out, "I just found out I'm pregnant. I haven't told anyone, not even my folks. What am I going to do?"

George Brown, a young and upcoming businessman, greets Fred Schwartz, an elder, following the Sunday morning worship service. George asks Fred if he can speak with him for a moment. They both move down the hall to a vacant classroom. As they enter the room George says, "You have been in business for many years and I thought you might be able to help me. I have the opportunity to enter into a very profitable business deal, but there are some questionable ethical issues involved and I need some advice."

Sally Jacobs, a young mother with three preschool

children, is sitting next to Joan DeLorenzo, a middle-aged mother of five teenagers, at a ladies missionary society meeting. Sally has known Joan for over a year and has come to enjoy her company. During a break in the program Sally turns to Joan and says, "I don't know how you managed with five children. Three are more than I can handle. I'm in over my head and I need help."

Carl Henry, well-known evangelical theologian, asks, "Suppose a Christian under emotional stress walked into a Christian group. How could its members help him?" He goes on to answer his own question by saying, "Ordinary laymen should be able to minister to one another at least on an elementary level. . . . All thoughtful help need not come from the pastor" (Henry 1980, 22).

As we think about Henry's answer, at least two questions come to mind. First, should lay people be involved in a counseling ministry? Is this an appropriate role for them? Second, can lay persons be effective counselors? We will examine these two questions more closely. First, we will deal with lay involvement in a counseling ministry.

LAITY AND MINISTRY

In popular usage the terms *laity* or *lay people* refer to nonprofessionals. For example, in the field of medicine, doctors and nurses are professionals while the rest of us are lay persons. In the field of law, lawyers are professionals, but doctors and nurses are lay persons. In the church, the clergy are considered the professionals while the laity are the nonprofessionals. However, it is important for us to understand how the Bible uses these terms.

The English word *laity* is a transliteration of the Greek word *laikos*, which means "belonging to the *laos*." The word *laos* is used 143 times in the New Testament and is usually translated "people."

In the four Gospels as well as the early chapters of Acts, *laos* generally refers to Israel or the Jewish people (e.g., Matt. 2:6; John 11:50). However, after the establishment of the church, in the rest of Acts and the Epistles, *laos* refers to the Christian community (e.g., Acts 18:10; Rom. 9:25; Titus 2:14; Heb. 4:9; 1 Pet. 2:9). The church is the *laos* or people of God. Whereas the Jews were referred to as the people of God in the Old Testament, the church is seen as the people of God in the New Testament (e.g., Rom. 2:28-29; Gal. 6:16; 1 Pet. 2:10) (Kittel 1967, 4:29-57).

Furthermore, every time the word *laos* is used of Christians in the New Testament it refers to all the believers. It is never used to distinguish between ordinary believers and a priestly or ministerial class. According to the New Testament all of us, as believers, make up the *laos* or people of God.

We may best understand the status of the laity as full and equal members and participants in the church and its ministry by what is commonly known as the doctrine of the priesthood of the believer. This doctrine received its fullest treatment through Martin Luther's study of the second chapter of First Peter.

The major theme of First Peter deals with how to handle persecution that results from living as a Christian in a pagan world. Peter points out that Christians are in a special relationship to God. He uses words such as *elect* (1:2), *called* (1:15; 2:9, 21; 3:9; 5:10), and *chosen* (1:2; 2:4, 9; 5:13). This election, calling, and choice is based on the atonement provided by Jesus Christ (1:2-5, 19-21; 3:18). Believers are able to handle persecution and to suffer, even as Christ did, through faith in God's plan of salvation. Because we have faith in Christ and His atonement we know that we are God's elect, called, and chosen and have direct access to God. First Peter 2:4-10 is a proclamation of all Christians as the *laos* of God, a holy and royal priesthood who serve God in handling persecution and suffering.

According to this passage all believers are priests before God. Each of us has equal access to God and there is no need for another person to mediate between us and God. Commenting on the *royal priesthood* (2:5, 9), Luther says, "It would please me very much if this word 'priest' were used as commonly as the term 'Christian' is applied to us. For priests, the baptized, and Christians are all one and the same" (Pelikan and Mansen 1967, 30:63).

What is the role of the laity, this holy and royal priesthood? At least two roles are readily evident in this passage. The first, according to 1 Peter 2:5, is to offer spiritual sacrifices. This relates to worship. Each of us as Christians is to be involved in worship. Since we each have direct access to God, we are to use that access for worship as we bring our *spiritual sacrifices*. The second role, according to 1 Peter 2:9, is to declare the promises of God. Not only are we to worship God, we are also to proclaim the good news that all may become priests by faith in Christ.

Howard Snyder has suggested a third role growing out of this passage on the priesthood of the believer, that of being priests to each other. He points out that many persons understand the priesthood of the believer only in terms of direct access to God. While this is of course true, the priesthood of the believer involves more than access to God. "It also means that if we are a priesthood we are priests to each other. We are a fellowship. We are a community of God's people" (Snyder 1980, 4).

The idea of all believers ministering to each other as members of the *laos* of God is integral to the New Testament teaching on gifts. First Corinthians 12:4-11 teaches that the Holy Spirit has given all of us gifts so that we may minister to the community—the *laos*— the body of

Christ, and through this community of believers to the world at large.

There are three primary New Testament passages that deal with gifts. They are Romans 12:3-8, 1 Corinthians 12:4-30, and Ephesians 4:7-13. It is evident from these passages that each member of the body of Christ has gifts. However, no believer has all the gifts (1 Cor. 12:27-30).

Another teaching of these passages on the gifts is that they are not primarily for personal edification but for ministry to the Christian community and through it to the world. As Paul says, *so in Christ we who are many form one body, and each member belongs to all the others* (Rom. 12:5, NIV). He later says, *to each man the manifestation of the Spirit is given for the common good* (1 Cor. 12:7, NIV), and *to each one of us grace has been given . . . to prepare God's people for works of service, so that the body of Christ may be built up* (Eph. 4:7, 12). New Testament Christianity places a strong emphasis on relationships.

It is also clear in these passages on gifts that the emphasis is on unity and oneness. There is no indication of any hierarchical structure. The emphasis is unmistakably on a common membership in the body of Christ and interdependence. Each one of us is important and indispensable. If one member is missing all suffer; if one member exercises his or her gift all benefit. While the gifts are given to us as individuals they belong to the church as a whole. Each of us is called to minister.

If the New Testament teaches that the laity and the clergy have the same status as *laos*, or the people of God, as well as priests before God and the same role of ministering to each other and the world, then what is the distinction between what we popularly call the laity and the clergy? A number of writers suggest that the major distinction is that the clergy have been called to full-time ministry and have received advanced professional training. These writers see the major task of the clergy as one of equipping the laity for ministry (Butler et al.). This equipping is not to make the laity assistants to the clergy but rather partners with the clergy.

If all believers are gifted for ministry and are expected to exercise their gifts, then the major responsibility of the professional clergy is to enable lay ministry. In Matthew 28:19-20, Jesus instructed His disciples to go and make other disciples and to teach them what they had learned from Him. Christ did not expect us Christians to mature naturally or mystically as we acquired the skills needed to minister. He recognized we would need to be instructed and equipped so He commanded His disciples to continue the enabling ministry He had begun with them.

Second Timothy 2:2 reads, *The things you have heard me say in the presence of many witnesses entrust to reliable men who will also be qualified to teach others.* A significant part of the Pastoral Epistles is devoted to the instructing of young pastors in enabling lay ministry.

Paul calls the believers at Philippi partners with him in the ministry of the gospel (Phil. 1:5). As partners with the clergy lay persons should be involved in any ministry that their abilities, gifts, and training permit (Eph. 4:11-12). This includes the ministry of counseling. The New Testament passages dealing with a counseling ministry are addressed to all believers, not just church leaders (e.g., Gal. 6:1-2; 1 Thess. 5:14).

EFFECTIVENESS OF LAY COUNSELING

The second question raised at the beginning of this chapter is, Can lay persons be effective counselors? This is an important question because many lay persons get involved in counseling whether they realize it or not. The

Sunday school teacher who is asked for advice by a student is seen as a counselor. The lay person whose neighbor shares a marital problem may become involved in counseling. The elder who visits a sick parishioner in the hospital is a potential counselor. Parents often engage in counseling with their children. In fact, the first question raised—Should lay persons engage in counseling?—is almost irrelevant. Most lay people cannot avoid being involved in counseling. The second question—Can lay persons be effective counselors?—is critical.

The term *counseling* should be defined before the effectiveness of lay counseling can be considered. *Counseling* is a somewhat structured, healing relationship for the purpose of dealing with a problem or crisis in the life of an individual or individuals. Counseling is distinguished from psychotherapy in that psychotherapy generally deals with deeper emotional problems and involves long-term treatment. Counseling generally deals with normal people involved in the problems and crises of life. Counseling usually deals with the immediate and therefore tends to be of shorter duration and is less intensive than psychotherapy (McLemore 1974, 50-54). Most counseling falls into one of two areas—guidance counseling or crisis counseling. These are dealt with in later chapters.

The effectiveness of lay counseling is an issue that has been well researched. Lay counselors, often referred to as nonprofessionals or paraprofessionals, have been used in the field of mental health for years. Gerard Egan, a professor of psychology at Loyola University of Chicago, reports sixteen different research studies which demonstrate that lay counselors with some training can be as effective as professional counselors in dealing with many types of problems (Egan 1975, 9). Lawrence Brammer, a psychology professor at the University of Washington, has found that lay persons with the natural ability and some basic counseling skills can often be as effective as professional counselors (Brammer 1973, 10-12). Francine Sobey, a professor of social work at Columbia University, reports on a large-scale research project by the National Institute of Mental Health. Almost all of the directors of the mental health centers studied felt that properly trained paraprofessionals were effective counselors (Sobey 1970, 153-54).

It appears then that lay persons can be effective counselors. However, the one point that all the researchers cited above stress is that effectiveness involves training in basic counseling skills. This manual is designed to be part of such a training program. It is our belief that all Christians should have a basic knowledge of counseling skills because each of us eventually does some counseling, even within the home. An essential aspect of the people of God is their relationship with each other as brothers and sisters. Counseling skills provide the basis for turning this bond into a healing relationship. Some of you will find that your abilities and personal characteristics lend themselves to counseling and you may want to have a broader counseling ministry. In that case you will need to develop further the skills discussed in this manual. Whether or not you decide to become more actively involved in counseling, we hope the concepts and skills presented in this manual will enrich your Christian life and walk.

DISCUSSION QUESTIONS

1. *Think about some of the opportunities you have had to counsel. Were you aware you were in a counseling situation? Did you feel that you could handle the situation?*
2. *Do you agree with Carl Henry's comment on the importance of lay ministry? Why?*

3. What is your reaction to Howard Snyder's suggestion, on page 14, that the priesthood of the believer involves each of us being priests to each other?
4. Did the research findings that lay counselors, in many situations, are as effective as professional counselors surprise you? Why?
5. What do you anticipate gaining from this manual?

SUGGESTED READING

Brammer, Lawrence M. *The Helping Relationship.* Englewood Cliffs, N.J.: Prentice-Hall, 1973. A readable basic text on lay counseling. It gives a practical discussion on the nature of peer helping, characteristics of helpers, the helping relationship, and basic helping skills.

Collins, Gary. *How to Be a People Helper.* Santa Ana, Cal.: Vision House, 1976. A readable lay counseling manual by a popular Christian psychologist. Written from an evangelical perspective with an emphasis on basic skills. Its weakness is its lack of theological and theoretical basis.

Egan, Gerard. *The Skilled Helper.* Monterey, Cal.: Brooks/Cole, 1975. A model for lay counseling with interesting case material. Basic skills related to the model are presented.

Miller, Paul M. *Peer Counseling in the Church.* Scottdale, Pa.: Herald, 1978. A discussion of the role and effectiveness of lay counselors in the church. It also considers counselor characteristics and counseling skills. While written from a Christian perspective, it is weak on theology.

Welter, Paul. *How to Help a Friend.* Wheaton: Tyndale, 1978. A consideration of counseling with friends. Written by an evangelical, it develops an interesting but somewhat complex model. Again, the theological basis is weak.

CHAPTER TWO

Theology for Counseling

Two teenage girls were discussing possible careers. One of the girls commented, "My brother wants to be a great theologian when he grows up." The other girl replied, "Frankly, I think he would make a wonderful theologian." "Why?" asked the first girl. "Because," responded the second, "nobody can understand a word he says."

We laugh at this story because many people think of theology as a deep philosophical discipline. They believe theologians use long words and speak so that ordinary people cannot understand. While some aspects of theology do involve deep philosophical issues and some theologians do use big words and speak so that most people (sometimes even other theologians) cannot understand, theology is relevant to all Christians. Reduced to its basic meaning, theology is what one understands and believes about God and His work. Each of us has a theology that influences our views of the rest of life. If we are going to become involved in the ministry of counseling, we need to develop our theology in those areas related to counseling.

As Christians we look to the Bible to learn about God and His work. While God has revealed information about

Himself in His creation, His Word is the primary source of revelation for us. As we develop a theology for counseling we want to look at the Scriptures to see what they have to say about counseling. We also want to see what the Bible has to say about the essence of human nature as well as the effects of the Fall and redemption on human nature. We need to have a sound theological basis on which to build a theory of counseling. It is our theology and theory of counseling that will guide our use of counseling skills and techniques.

THE BIBLE AND COUNSELING

The Bible has a good deal to say about the ministry of counseling. We want to examine some of the major passages dealing with counseling so that we can understand the biblical ideas and principles of this ministry. Counseling is not a ministry of modern origin or a new fad. Its practice is recorded in both the Old and New Testaments. Jesus Christ Himself had an extensive counseling ministry as recorded in the Gospels. God has worked through people in the ministry of counseling for centuries.

OLD TESTAMENT

As we examine the Old Testament Scriptures we find they have a great deal to say about the ministry of counseling. One of the earliest accounts of counseling in Scripture is found in Exodus 18:5-26. In this passage Jethro, Moses' father-in-law, came to visit Moses in the wilderness. First Jethro listened to Moses as he recounted all that had taken place since he had last seen Jethro (18:8-11). Then Jethro observed Moses caring for his responsibilities with the people of Israel. Jethro saw that Moses had taken on too much responsibility (18:17-18).

However, before giving Moses any advice, he first asked him about his responsibilities (18:14). When he had given Moses an opportunity to explain (18:15-16), Jethro gave him a suggestion on how to handle the situation (18:19-23). Moses followed his father-in-law's counsel because it was wisely delivered (18:24-26).

The Hebrew word translated "advice" (NIV) or "counsel" (AV and RSV) is *ya'ats* and means advice in the form of guidance or direction. This same word is used in 1 Kings 12:9, 28 where Rehoboam seeks counsel on how to answer the people who have come to his coronation seeking relief from heavy conscription and taxes. The same word is also found in Proverbs 13:10, *wisdom is found in those who take advice.*

The Book of Proverbs speaks frequently of the benefit of advice or counsel. The word most often used in this book is *etsah* which is derived from *ya'ats* and has basically the same meaning. Proverbs 12:15 reads, *A wise man listens to advice.* The same idea is found in Proverbs 19:20. Proverbs 20:18 says, *Make plans by seeking advice.* This usage of *etsah* refers to what is called guidance counseling, an important aspect of the ministry of lay counseling.

In Psalm 55:13-14, David talks about how much he had enjoyed the counsel of a friend, one who was an equal (peer counseling). David called it *sweet counsel* (AV). The word used here for counsel is *cowd* which is derived from a root meaning "to consult," and by implication confidential or private counsel (Strong 1980). It is interesting to note that David was betrayed by this friend (55:12-13). Based on David's choice of word for "counsel," it has been suggested that this betrayal involved breaking the confidence of the counseling relationship (Wright 1977, 22).

The above passages are illustrative of the place of counseling in the Old Testament. These passages teach us that the ministry of counseling is important and that the wise person seeks counsel. The Old Testament provides us with some important insights that we need to consider as we develop an approach to counseling.

NEW TESTAMENT

The New Testament addresses the ministry of counseling even more fully than the Old. Dr. Frank Minirth, a Christian psychiatrist, points out that there are at least five verbs in the New Testament that refer to the ministry of counseling: *parakaleo, noutheteo, paramutheomai, antechomai,* and *makrothumeo* (Minirth 1977, 37). We will examine the specific meaning of each of these verbs in order to understand what they have to say about the ministry of counseling.

The word *parakaleo* has four basic meanings or uses in the New Testament. One meaning is the act of asking for help. This use is limited to the first three Gospels (e.g., Matt. 8:5; Mark 5:18; Luke 7:4). A second meaning is exhortation in the sense of speaking, for God, to people. It is particularly used in the sense of exhorting people in well doing, a word of encouragement or prodding. This usage is found in Acts and the Pauline Epistles (e.g., Acts 14:22; 2 Cor. 5:20; Phil. 4:2). Another meaning is consoling help in the sense of a word of consolation or comfort. This usage is found in the Pauline Epistles and Hebrews (e.g., Rom. 15:4; 2 Thess. 2:16; Heb. 12:5). The fourth meaning is that of comfort by individuals, but offered in God's place, recognizing that all comfort ultimately comes from God although He works through people. This usage is limited to the Pauline Epistles (e.g., 2 Cor. 1:3-4; 2:7; 1 Thess. 4:18) (Kittel, 5:794). Summarizing the New Testament usage of *parakaleo* we find that it refers to Christians helping, exhorting, consoling, and comforting each other for God.

The second New Testament word, *noutheteo*, means to admonish or correct, but in such a way as not to provoke or embitter the person being corrected (e.g., Eph. 6:4) (Kittel, 4:1021). This word has the connotation of confrontation. At times people need to be confronted; they need to face up to a situation and consider their behavior. However, this confrontation is to be carried out in love and gentleness. The object is to help others, not to offend or hurt them.

The literal meaning of *paramutheomai*, according to Kittel's *Theological Dictionary of the New Testament*, is "to speak to someone, coming close to his side" (Kittel, 5:817). In its New Testament usage *paramutheomai* actually takes on a twofold meaning, admonition and comfort. However, these two aspects are inseparable. Admonition becomes comfort and comfort becomes admonition. The idea is that one is admonished in such a way that one is comforted by it.

The fourth word, *antechomai*, appears only four times in the New Testament (Matt. 6:24; Luke 16:13; 1 Thess. 5:14; Titus 1:9). The literal meaning of *antechomai* is to hold fast or hold tight to, and by implication in one's own interest. The word is used in this sense in all of the above passages except 1 Thessalonians 5:14. In this verse it appears to be used in a figurative sense meaning to hold on with more concern for the interest of the other than one's own (Kittel, 2:827). As Christian counselors, we must be willing to put the interest of the counselee before our own in the counseling situation.

The last word is *makrothumeo*. We usually find this word translated "longsuffering" or "patience" (1 Cor. 13: 4; Eph. 4:2). However, we need to realize that the New Testament concept of longsuffering or patience is more than endurance or indulgence, it is spiritual power which arises from the longsuffering of God (Kittel, 4:384). The Christian counselor needs to practice a patience that goes beyond human effort and relies on the power of God.

All five of these counseling words are found in 1 Thessalonians 5:14: *And we urge* ₍parakaleo₎ *you, brothers, warn* ₍noutheteo₎ *those who are idle, encourage* ₍paramutheomai₎ *the timid, help* ₍antechomai₎ *the weak, be patient* ₍makrothumeo₎ *with everyone.* This verse is part of a passage dealing with relationships in the church. Relationships between the leaders and the congregation are dealt with in verses 12 and 13, while relationships among all believers are dealt with in verses 14 and 15.

Two important insights are found in verse 14 that are applicable to the ministry of counseling. First, this verse is addressed to all believers. Each of us as believers, and not just the leaders, is to be involved in exhorting, encouraging, comforting, and helping—in short, counseling. All believers are to exercise warm, loving concern for each other. Second, different people need different forms of counseling. Some need to be confronted, exhorted, or admonished while others need to be comforted or helped. There is not one approach to counseling, but a variety of approaches depending on an individual's needs and circumstances. We see in this verse the importance of a well-rounded and flexible approach to counseling for meeting the needs of our brothers and sisters. When needs are met by such concern and skill, Christians experience the joy of healing relationships.

Another New Testament passage that helps us understand the ministry of counseling is Galatians 6:1-2.

Brothers, if someone is caught in a sin, you who are spiritual should restore him gently. But watch yourself, or you also may be tempted. Carry each other's burdens, and in this way you will fulfill the law of Christ.

The Epistle to the Galatians deals with freedom from the Old Testament law through faith in Christ. In the first four chapters of this epistle the argument for freedom from the law through Christ is presented. In the last two chapters living with freedom in Christ is dealt with. That life is to be lived, not by following the law, but by the indwelling Spirit (5:16-25). Galatians 6:1-2 comes in the middle of this second section.

We see that an evidence of a Spirit-filled walk is concern for fellow believers. This concern should lead to action. Those *who are spiritual* need to be ready to reach out to others, to help restore those who have strayed, and to help others with the burdens of life. This is the essence of Christian love, one of the fruits of the Spirit.

Several other New Testament passages teach us the same basic concepts that have been discovered in the above passages (e.g., Rom. 12:15; 15:14; 1 Cor. 4:14; 2 Cor. 1:3-4; 1 Thess. 4:18). The one thing all these passages have in common is that they are addressed to all believers, to the whole community, and not just to the leaders or some other select group. It is apparent that in the New Testament, counseling is a ministry for all the people of God; each one of us is to be involved.

COUNSELING MINISTRY OF JESUS

Our discussion of counseling in the New Testament would not be complete without looking at the counseling ministry of Jesus. As John Drakeford points out, Jesus was not a psychologist by training or practice. However, Jesus had an effective counseling ministry because He understood people, He related well to them, and He listened to them; in other words, He used the methods now followed by modern counselors (Drakeford 1961, 10).

Frank Minirth suggests that there are six areas in which Jesus excelled in His counseling ministry. First, He had perfect insight into the problems of individuals (John 2:25). Second, He made good use of questions (e.g.,

Luke 10:26; 18:19; John 4:7, NIV). Third, Jesus had genuine concern for those He counseled (e.g., Mark 10:21). Fourth, He maintained a close relationship with the Father (e.g., Matt. 14:23; Mark 1:35; Luke 5:16; 6:12; John 17). Fifth, He knew the solutions to people's problems and could help individuals discover these solutions (e.g., Luke 19:1-10; John 3:1-21). Finally, Jesus used a balanced approach. He knew when to be confrontative and when to be nondirective (Minirth 1977, 192-93).

Norman Wright, professor of counseling at Biola University, states, "Jesus' ministry was that of helping people achieve fullness of life, assisting them develop an ability to deal with the problems and conflicts and burdens of life" (Wright 1977, 25). Wright then goes on to list eleven characteristics or techniques of Jesus' counseling ministry: (1) compassion, (2) acceptance of others, (3) recognition of the worth of others, (4) seeing others as responsible, (5) communicating hope, encouragement, and inspiration, (6) emphasizing peace of mind, (7) teaching or communicating information, (8) expressing Himself authoritatively, (9) seeing individuals' needs and addressing them, (10) emphasizing right behavior, and (11) flexibility in dealing with people in different ways and at different levels of depth or closeness (Wright 1977, 26-28).

The New Testament demonstrates that Jesus had a counseling ministry and that He modeled the principles of counseling found both in the Old and New Testaments (Luke 4:18). A study of the counseling ministry of Jesus is instructive in the development of a theology of counseling.

Summarizing the scriptural teaching on counseling, we see that this ministry has a prominent role to play in the life of the church. The New Testament emphasis is that counseling is a ministry that each one of us is to be engaged in and that it is not reserved for a privileged few. The New Testament also teaches that there are a variety of approaches to counseling, based on the needs of the counselee, but that all approaches center on our relationship to God through Jesus Christ. Finally, Jesus has modeled for us a counseling ministry for the church, demonstrating the principles inherent in Scripture.

THE ESSENCE OF HUMAN NATURE: CREATION, THE FALL, AND REDEMPTION

Wright points us toward the starting point in developing an approach to counseling when he says:

The starting place for developing a method of counseling or helping others is not the consideration of specific techniques but rather a focus upon the nature of God and the nature of man. . . . How we view man— who he is, his potentials and his defects—certainly influences how we respond to individuals within the context of counseling (Wright 1977, 19).

CREATION

One of the passages dealing with the creation of humans is Genesis 2:7, *And the Lord God formed man from the dust of the ground and breathed into his nostrils the breath of life, and man became a living being.* It has been suggested that *dust* symbolizes the material aspect of humanity while *breath* symbolizes the immaterial aspect of humanity (Keil 1949, 1:78).

Genesis 1:26-28 teaches that humans are created in the image of God. This, most likely, does not refer to humans' material or physical dimensions because God is spirit (John 4:24). On their physical side humans resemble the rest of God's animal creation. Humans share many of the same biological characteristics as animals. Ronald Koteskey, a professor of psychology at Asbury College, points out that to understand the essence of human nature we must take into account the similarities between humans and the animals.

Koteskey reminds us that the study of comparative anatomy and physiology aids in understanding these similarities. Comparative anatomy reveals the structural similarities between humans and other animals, particularly primates. Comparative physiology reveals that many of the same biochemical reactions take place in both animals and humans. This is what makes it possible for drugs and other medical techniques to be tested on animals before they are tried on humans. The human sensory apparatus is also similar to that of animals. In fact, a major portion of the scientific understanding of the functioning of the eyes and ears comes from animal studies. The physiological mechanisms of the endocrine system which underlie drives such as hunger and thirst are similar in humans and animals. Through animal studies we are better able to understand how changes and malfunctions in the endocrine system affect human behavior (Koteskey 1980, 87).

In attempting to understand human behavior as well as in counseling with individuals it is important that we be aware of physiological effects on human behavior. Diet, sleep, drugs, abnormal functioning of various physiological systems, or other biological factors have great significance. The physiological factors should not be overlooked when evaluating or trying to understand individual human behavior. The human body is subject to the same weaknesses and frailties as animals. It is important to keep in mind that humans, like animals, are finite creatures.

While humans are similar to animals in some ways, they are qualitatively distinct from them in other ways.

This qualitative distinction results from humans being made *in the image of God*. The image of God refers to the ability to relate to God as beings who in some limited way share aspects of His essence. What is the aspect of God in us that allows us to relate to Him and each other? Theologians suggest it involves self-consciousness, reason or rationality, and responsibility. Francis Schaeffer sums up these characteristics in the term "personality" (Schaeffer 1968, 87).

The concept of personality is important to the development of both a theology for counseling and a theory of counseling. We will define personality as that essence of human nature that is self-aware, aware of others, capable of relating to others, capable of reason and reflection, morally responsible, and spiritual. Personality also involves the traits and characteristics that make our behavior relatively consistent.

We believe that the central aspect of human personality is reason and responsibility. God created us with the ability to reason so that we could relate to God. Responsibility grows out of reason. God created us as rational beings in order to relate to Him. We are responsible to our Creator. God has created us with the capability to respond to Him and we are responsible to do so.

THE FALL

While humans were created in the image of God to be able to relate to Him, that relationship was affected by rebellion against God. What effect did this rebellion, referred to as the Fall, have on that relationship with God and on the image of God?

God's relationship with humans was not completely severed because of the Fall, but it was drastically altered. Humans no longer had direct access to God. They had to communicate through mediators—priests to speak to

God for them and prophets to speak to them for God. Sacrifices were necessary to atone for acts of rebellion (sins). God's relationship with His people was, for the most part, formal and distant.

While several of the church fathers, as well as some contemporary theologians, see the Fall as completely destroying the image of God in humanity, we agree with many theologians who see the image as marred rather than destroyed. It is interesting to note that humans have not lost their power to dominate creation, although it has been made more difficult. Humans have not lost their ability to hear and respond to God. In Genesis 3:14-19, we see that all creation fell with humanity. Romans 8:18-22 speaks of the effects of the Fall on nature. Yet, in spite of the Fall, the apostle Paul could say that God could be seen in nature (Rom. 1:20). In the same way the image of God survives in humanity.

Sin and the Fall have had consequences for all humans; each one of us has been affected. Emil Brunner, a Reformed theologian, sees the direct consequence of the Fall and human sin as being a distortion in humanity's sense of direction. He argues that God had set the direction for humans, but they sought to become gods themselves and to set their own direction. Because of the Fall our tendency is now to look to ourselves and the world for direction rather than to God (Brunner 1952, 125-28).

According to Brunner, humanity's desire to be its own god and set its own direction leads to an internal conflict. This conflict is between our desire to direct ourselves and our need to be directed by God. This conflict, then, results in four basic psychological problems. The first is despair. People feel a need for God's direction in their lives but they set up legalistic religious codes, false religions, instead. When they fail to live up to these codes they experience despair. In the seventh chapter of Romans, Paul teaches that separation from God leads to legalism which in turn leads to despair.

Mark Cosgrove and James Mallory explain this human dilemma by saying, " . . . man aspires to good because he is created in God's image, but it is impossible for man not to 'sin' because he is born alienated from God, and thus is self-centered at birth" (Cosgrove and Mallory 1977, 27). Humans need the power to overcome sin and to heal their relationship with God. It is only as individuals become reconciled to God that they can fully overcome despair.

The second psychological problem seen by Brunner as arising from this internal conflict is unrest or lack of peace. We find our completeness in God and without Him there is a restlessness. Humans restlessly search for completeness while their self-deification keeps them from coming to God. Completeness and real peace can only be found in a right relationship with God.

Guilt is the third psychological problem resulting from this sin-created internal conflict. In counseling we find two types of guilt: false and real. By false guilt we mean guilt arising from behavior that may not be wrong but the individual believes is wrong. False guilt is often produced by family, friends, and one's subculture. An individual may experience guilt over a specific act because the individual has been taught some behavior is wrong. If, in fact, the behavior is not wrong, then the individual experiences false guilt. False guilt may also arise when one feels something is wrong even if he has not been so taught. False guilt needs to be dealt with by getting at the source of the guilt and by correcting the beliefs of the individual. The Bible gives us a basis for this re-education process.

While many people experience false guilt, there is real or genuine guilt. We stand guilty before God and in need of His forgiveness. The good news is that there is forgiveness to deal with real guilt. Guilt can incapacitate a person and can lead to serious mental problems. Guilt is one of the most debilitating emotions. As Christians we have in the Word of God the answer to guilt. The Bible offers correction for the faulty thinking that leads to false guilt and contains the message of forgiveness for real guilt.

The fourth psychological problem resulting from this internal conflict is anxiety. Anxiety is an underlying feeling that something is wrong. It is a constant worry that seems to have no basis. This anxiety results from the tension between what we could be and what we are. God, in creation, gave us tremendous potential. That potential has been thwarted by sin resulting from our desire to run our own lives. It is only when we have a right relationship with God and allow Him to set the direction for our lives that this conflict can be reduced, and our anxiety overcome; then we can more fully realize our potential.

Reuel Howe, a pastor and seminary professor, sees the consequences of the Fall and sin in terms of alienation (Howe 1952, 38-46). He suggests there are three ways this alienation is experienced. First, there is the alienation from oneself, self-rejection. This alienation from oneself, according to Howe, results from the contrast between what one is and what one might have been. In our attempt to overcome this alienation we compensate with various strategies such as materialism, narcissism, sexism, racism, and others. All of these strategies are doomed to failure and result in psychological problems. This alienation from self can only be overcome when we are in right relationship with our Creator.

The second way one experiences alienation is alienation from others. Howe sees one's alienation from others growing out of one's alienation from self; self-rejection leads to rejection of others. In discussing people's alienation from others, he makes a profound statement, "God created persons to be loved and things to be used." He goes on to say that instead, "we are always tempted to love things and use people" (Howe 1952, 24). Howe believes people love things as a substitute for human relationships because things do not make demands on them or hurt them. On the other hand, people tend to use others to meet the needs growing out of their self-alienation.

Using others takes at least two basic forms: deception and manipulation. Deception is the act of deceiving others, of leading them to believe something that is not so. Manipulation is a form of deception; it often involves hiding one's goal from another. Manipulation involves getting others to act on the basis of deception. Deception and manipulation may be practiced at both the conscious and unconscious levels. Counselors must be aware of the potential for deception and manipulation not only in their counselees, but also in themselves.

Alienation from others and the tendency to use them can only be overcome through acceptance of self which results from God's acceptance received by faith. Counselors need to realize that God has accepted them even though they also are deceptive and manipulative persons and He works with them to bring about change. It is this acceptance by God that allows counselors to accept their counselees as deceptive and manipulative and work with them to bring about change.

The third way one experiences alienation, suggests Howe, is in alienation from God. In fact, it is this alienation from God that is the source of our alienation from self and others. Because of all these alienations we tend to feel alone and anxious, unaccepted and unaccepting, and finally hostile and destructive. Howe goes on to point out that through Jesus Christ, God reached out to humankind with an offer of reconciliation. It is the atonement that makes reconciliation possible. It is through Christ that one can be reconciled to God, to oneself, and to one's neighbor.

REDEMPTION

While there was nothing humanity could do about the power of sin or do to be reconciled to God, He was able to make a way of reconciliation. The apostle Paul tells us,

Therefore, if anyone is in Christ, he is a new creation; the old has gone, the new has come! All this is from God who reconciled us to himself through Christ and gave us the ministry of reconciliation: that God was reconciling the world to himself in Christ, not counting men's sins against them. And he has committed to us the message of reconciliation. We are therefore Christ's ambassadors, as though God were making his appeal through us. We implore you on Christ's behalf: Be reconciled to God. God made him who had no sin to be sin for us, so that in him we might become the right-eousness of God (2 Cor. 5:17-21).

In these verses we see that we are reconciled to God through Christ. The old creation was marred by sin so we are recreated or in Paul's words have become a *new creation*. We have been accepted by God, not because we deserve it, but because Christ took our sins on Himself. The basis of our reconcilation is grace, God's unmerited favor toward us (Eph. 2:8-9). Our reconciliation is a free gift. Because we have been reconciled we have been given the ministry of reconciliation.

Reuel Howe suggests that we have three basic needs that are met through the reconciling work of God in Christ (Howe 1952, 105-41). The first is the need for love. The true source of love is God (1 John 4:10). It is only as one responds to God's love that one is truly able to love oneself and others. This truth is especially relevant for Christian counselors. It is because we have been loved and forgiven by God that we are able to accept the shortcomings and failings of our counselees and love them (Eph. 4:32). God's love becomes incarnate in the Christian counselor (1 John 4:12). The Christian counselor, in Howe's words, is, "to be forgiven and forgiving; to be reconciled and reconciling; to be loved and loving" (Howe 1952, 97).

The second need suggested by Howe is acceptance. We are able to accept others because God has accepted us. God accepts us as we are. God did not send Christ to die for our sins after we turned to Him, but while we were still rebellious sinners (Rom. 5:6-10; 1 John 4:9-10). God accepts us as we are and works with us to change. We are redeemed in order to do good, not by being good or winning God's acceptance (Eph. 2:8-10). In the same way as Christian counselors we can accept others as they are and work with them. We accept others with the acceptance God has given us. Acceptance is a key to healing relationships.

The third need met by the reconciling work of God in Christ, Howe suggests, is discipline. He defines discipline not in terms of rules and punishment, but in terms of boundaries for protection and guidance. He sees these boundaries as the source of true human freedom.

Paradoxically there can be no freedom, but only anarchy, without boundaries. We were created to function within boundaries. Freedom involves choice and it is only when we choose to follow God, to live within the boundaries He has set, that we find fulfillment and meaning. The Christian counselor needs to recognize the human need for discipline, which involves God's guidance and protection, in working with counselees.

As we reflect on the implications of the Fall and redemption for a counseling ministry, it seems clear that sinfulness is at the root of human problems. Therefore a major step in solving a person's problems would be to have that person be reconciled to God through Christ.

Effective counseling begins with a basic understanding of the essence of human nature. We need to recognize that humans are creatures who have a physical dimension that affects their behavior. They are also spiritual beings, made in the image of God. We must understand the full effects of the Fall and sin on the image of God in humanity and on human behavior. However, we must also realize the potential for humanity in the reconciling work of God in Christ Jesus. A biblical concept of the essence of human nature—created by God, affected by the Fall, and renewed by redemption—provides us with a basis for a theory of lay counseling.

DISCUSSION QUESTIONS

1. *What do you believe about God and His work? How do those beliefs affect your everyday life?*
2. *Why should Christians have a sound theological basis for every type of ministry?*
3. *In what ways was Jethro an effective counselor?*
4. *What insights or principles did you gain from the New Testament passages on counseling?*
5. *What implications for counseling do you see in the discussion of the essence of human nature, the Fall, and redemption?*

SUGGESTED READING

Carter, John D. and Narramore, Bruce. *The Integration of Psychology and Theology*. Grand Rapids: Zondervan, 1979. A book based on the assumption that both theology and psychology can help us better understand ourselves and others. It attempts to integrate the understandings of both subjects using the Bible as a final authority.

Collins, Gary. *The Rebuilding of Psychology*. Wheaton:

Tyndale, 1977. Another attempt to integrate psychology with a Christian perspective. This book presents a good critique of the major schools of psychology, discussing the strengths and weaknesses of each. The author concludes that a Christian approach to psychology must be centered on the Word of God.

Cosgrove, Mark P. *The Essence of Human Nature.* Grand Rapids: Zondervan, 1977. A discussion of the inadequacy of psychological views of human nature that do not account for our spiritual nature. The author examines the problems faced by those who see humans as material beings, or only as higher animals. The author presents a view of human nature consistent with psychological research and the Bible.

Cosgrove, Mark P. and Mallory, James D., Jr. *Mental Health: A Christian Approach.* Grand Rapids: Zondervan, 1977. An examination of the central elements in a Christian approach to mental health and psychotherapy. It discusses the sources of mental problems and the goals of therapy.

Crabb, Lawrence J., Jr. *Basic Principles of Biblical Counseling.* Grand Rapids: Zondervan, 1975. A good discussion of the essence of human nature, including particularly the effects of the Fall and sin. An attempt is made to develop a model for counseling that deals with human responsibility and rationality.

CHAPTER THREE

Theory for Lay Counseling: Relationship

A college professor asked a student to define the word *theory*. The student replied, "It is taking what everybody knows is true and putting it in words nobody can understand." Like theology, theory is often thought of as being complicated and often irrelevant to the "real" world. However, as theology is basically what we understand and believe about God and His work, so in the same way, theory is basically what one understands about some aspect of reality. It has to do with our understanding of how things work, why they work the way they do, and what, if anything, we can do to effect change. For example, the theory of gravity is basically a statement of beliefs about the attraction of the earth (and other large masses) on matter. As we study something we draw conclusions, which are called theories. As in other fields of study, theories have been developed in the areas of psychology and counseling.

It is important to have a theory on which to base our ministry of counseling. Paul Welter, professor of counseling and educational psychology at Kearney State College, Nebraska, suggests six advantages of having a theory of counseling. First, a theory of counseling provides counselors with a set of guidelines and leads to consistency in practice. Second, a theory gives confidence, a sense of security, which creates a secure climate for counseling. Third, a theoretical perspective provides counselors with a basis for evaluating their effectiveness as well as providing guidelines for correcting or strengthening their counseling. Fourth, a theory helps keep counselors from making errors or harming others. Fifth, it helps counselors see the counseling relationship as a process rather than as a series of isolated encounters. It provides a bridge from one session to the next and moves the process toward a goal. Sixth, a theory guides a counselor in skill acquisition. It directs the counselor toward appropriate skills and directs their use (Welter 1978, 20-21).

It is not the purpose of this manual to develop a comprehensive theory of counseling, but rather to provide basic theoretical guidelines that may give direction for effective lay counseling. These guidelines will be built on the theological foundation provided by the previous chapter. This theoretical approach to counseling will be centered around three basic concepts. We call it the 3R approach: Relationship, Responsibility, and Religion.* These three concepts are the topics of chapters 3, 4, and 5.

Psychologists have tried to determine what aspects of the counseling process are the best predictors of counseling effectiveness. The available research shows that the relationship between the counselor and the counselee is a better predictor of effectiveness than either the theory of personality followed or the techniques used (Combs, et al. 1971, 4). Many leading authorities on lay counseling feel that the relation between the counselor

---

*By religion we mean a living faith based on a personal relationship with Jesus Christ, not a formal ecclesiastical system.

and counselee is the major key to an effective counseling ministry (Kennedy et al.). They believe that it is the relationship that facilitates healing. This relationship involves three elements: (1) the counselor, (2) the counselee, and (3) their interrelationship.

THE COUNSELOR

Even as the relationship between the counselor and counselee is the major key to counseling effectiveness, the counselor is the key to that relationship. Psychological researchers say that it is difficult to distinguish between effective and ineffective counselors based on the school of thought they follow, but they can be clearly distinguished based on their personal characteristics (Brammer 1973, 18). Another group of psychologists consider that the primary tool that counselors work with is themselves (Combs 1971, 5).

The literature on counseling suggests a number of personal characteristics associated with counselor effectiveness: self-awareness, empathy, effective listening, warmth, genuineness, trustworthiness, and flexibility.

SELF-AWARENESS

One of the characteristics associated with effective counseling is a high level of self-awareness or self-concept. One writer describes a person's self-concept as

the center of his universe, the frame of reference from which he makes his observations. It is his personal reality and the vantage point from which all else is observed and comprehended (Combs 1971, 41-42).

It is important for us to understand ourselves and the perspectives from which we view the world. In our discussion of the essence of human nature in chapter 2, self-awareness was presented as one of the aspects of the image of God in humans. While all humans are capable of self-awareness, some exercise this ability to a fuller extent than others. It is important that those who desire to have an effective counseling ministry continually exercise their self-awareness.

Brammer suggests that there are at least three areas in which self-awareness is important: self, values, and feelings. A good counselor "must be able to answer very clearly the question . . . 'Who am I?'" (Brammer 1973, 21). Knowing our strengths and weaknesses is one of the more important aspects of knowing ourselves. Until we are able to evaluate our own strengths and weaknesses it is difficult to evaluate those of others. We must be aware of our value systems, not only what our values are but how they are ranked, that is, which are most important and central. It is important for us to be aware of our values so we will neither project* our values on counselees, misinterpret the values of counselees, nor become judgmental. We also need to be aware of our feelings so that we may control them as well as not project them on to the counselee. Feelings are generally a by-product of our thoughts and actions and are therefore indicators of ourselves.

Self-awareness is important for counselors in order for them to be objective in their evaluation of their counselees and their situations. Jesus taught us the importance of self-awareness for the evaluation process when He gave the illustration of our need to remove the log from our own eye before attempting to remove the splinter from another's eye (Matt. 7:3-5). From a Christian perspective, we need to constantly be aware of the fact

---

*The word project in psychological usage refers to the tendency to attribute one's beliefs or feelings to others. See the discussion of projections in chapter 4, for further details.

that we are only sinners saved by grace. When we lose sight of our own weakness we lose the empathy to reach out to others in their weakness.

EMPATHY

Another characteristic of effective counselors is empathy. This characteristic is mentioned in counseling literature more often than any other. Empathy is the other side of self-awareness; it is other-awareness. Empathy is the ability to see things from the other person's perspective, to feel what the other feels. However, it goes beyond this to include the communication of that understanding to the other.

The writer of the Book of Hebrews attributes this characteristic to Christ when he writes, *For we do not have a high priest who is unable to sympathize with our weaknesses, but we have one who has been tempted in every way, just as we are—yet was without sin* (4:15). The Greek word translated "sympathize" is *sumpathees*. This word does not have the same meaning as the English word *sympathize*, which means "feel sorry for." Instead, this Greek word means to feel the same thing as another (Kittel 1967, 5:935-36). Someone has said, "Empathy is two hearts sharing the same load."

EFFECTIVE LISTENING

Being a good listener is related to empathy. In order to more fully understand another, one must be an effective listener. Several aspects of effective listening are suggested:

1.   Effective listening begins by indicating that one hears the other person's feelings and meanings.

2.   Effective listening involves establishing eye contact and posture which clearly indicates that one is

listening.

3. Effective listening involves attention to nonverbal clues such as the tone of voice, posture, gestures, and mannerisms.

4. Effective listening avoids nagging, criticizing, threatening, lecturing, and ridiculing.

5. Effective listening treats the other person as one would want to be treated.

6. Effective listening involves accepting the other person's feelings.

7. Effective listening involves hearing the other person's feelings and meanings and stating these so the other person feels understood. It provides a mirror for the other person to see himself more clearly.

8. Effective listening gives open responses that accurately state what the other person feels and means rather than closed responses which are judgmental or directive. An open response allows the other to continue talking openly and freely about the problem.

9. Effective listening avoids responses that ignore the other person's feelings by communicating that one has not really heard or understood.

10. Effective listening lets the other person attempt to resolve his problem. It resists the impulse to immediately impose solutions, but rather helps the other to think through the alternatives in the situation (Arvidson 1977).

The New Testament sums up effective listening this way: *Everyone should be quick to listen, slow to speak* (James 1:19). Jethro practiced effective listening in counseling with Moses (Exod. 18:5-26). Jesus also modeled effective listening when He dealt with the woman at the well (John 4:1-26) and with the two men on the road to Emmaus (Luke 24:13-35).

WARMTH

A fourth characteristic of those who are effective in counseling others is warmth, the expression of care and concern. It is a means by which empathy is communicated and effective listening is facilitated. Warmth was a characteristic of Jesus' ministry. It was His loving concern for people in trouble that attracted the multitudes to Him. Because we Christians have received care and concern from God, we are in a unique position to reach out to others with care and concern (Eph. 4:32; 1 John 4:7-21).

We need to communicate this warmth to counselees. This needs to be done, not only in words, but by our tone of voice, facial expression, and whole demeanor. A smile, a soft voice, and good eye contact can communicate more than words. It does no good for us to have empathy for others if we do not communicate it. Our total person should convey that we understand what is being said and that we care for the person who is talking.

GENUINENESS

Genuineness is a characteristic mentioned in the counseling literature almost as frequently as empathy. Genuineness combines the attributes of honesty and consistency. Counselors must be themselves to be effective. Obviously self-awareness is foundational to true genuineness. "The truly genuine person," according to Collins, "is . . . consistent in his values or attitudes, not defensive, aware of his own emotions, willing to share of himself and his own feelings" (Collins 1976, 34).

Genuineness is also related to the concept of sincerity. In 2 Corinthians 1:12, Paul claims to have been sincere in his dealings with the Corinthians; that is, he had been honest and open with them. The New Testament also instructs believers to be sincere in their ministry (Phil. 1:3-11, especially verse 10). While all Christians should be genuine, this characteristic is especially important for those engaged in a counseling ministry.

TRUSTWORTHINESS

Trustworthiness relates to the issue of confidentiality and to competence boundaries.

For a counselee to be free to share innermost feelings and most private thoughts he must have confidence in the counselor's trustworthiness. A counselor must have deep respect for the confidentiality of the counseling relationship. The Scriptures commend the person who can keep matters in confidence (Prov. 11:13; 21:23). The Scriptures also warn against confiding in untrustworthy persons (Prov. 20:19). In Psalm 55:14, David indicates his sense of betrayal when one he trusted broke his confidence.

Trustworthiness also relates to competence boundaries—the boundary between areas in which the counselor is competent and areas in which the counselor is not competent. To be trustworthy we need to understand the boundaries of our competency. If we are not competent in a counselee's problem area, we should be honest and refer the counselee to someone who is. Admitting that we are not competent in an area is not a sign of weakness, but rather of concern and love. We will deal with the referral process in chapter 13.

FLEXIBILITY

Flexibility is another important characteristic of effective counselors. Sometimes they need to get deeply involved in a situation; at other times they may need to stand apart as objective observers. Effective counselors are able to minister at many different levels depending on the needs of the counselee and the situation.

In our examination of the New Testament's teaching on counseling in chapter 2, we noted that different techniques and approaches are needed for various persons based on their needs and the situation (1 Thess. 5:14). Jesus modeled this flexibility in His earthly ministry. Not only did He deal with people in different ways, He also related to individuals at different levels of depth or closeness. We can note the differences in Jesus' encounters with Nicodemus (John 3:1-21), the woman at the well (John 4:5-42), and the two on the road to Emmaus (Luke 24:13-35).

We need to recognize that not all counselors possess each of these characteristics to the fullest extent. However, the more fully developed these characteristics are, the more effective the counselor's ministry will be.

We also must recognize that, while some persons may be more gifted than others and some may possess more of these characteristics naturally, all of these characteristics can be developed to various degrees. To be effective counselors, therefore, we need to be committed to our own growth and development.

In the discussion of spiritual gifts in the previous chapter, we saw that while all believers are gifted, not all believers have every gift or the same gifts. However, the lack of a gift in an area need not exclude one from some ministering in that area. For example, a Christian who does not have the gift of evangelism (Eph. 4:11) should still be involved in evangelism as the opportunity arises, although that one should not make evangelism a primary ministry. In the same way, not all of us will manifest the characteristics of an effective counselor to the same degree, yet all of us should be prepared to counsel as opportunities arise. However, all of us should honestly evaluate ourselves in light of these characteristics, as well as our effectiveness in counseling, to determine whether counseling should be a primary or secondary ministry for us.

THE COUNSELEE

Two counselee attributes are essential for a healing relationship to develop. The first attribute is that the counselee must be aware of the existence of a problem. If the counselee does not feel a need for change or help, he or she is unlikely to seek counseling. The counselor may see needs or problems in the counselee, but unless the counselee sees or feels those needs, effective counseling is not likely to take place.

A second attribute that is necessary for effective counseling is that the counselee must want help for the problem. As Gary Collins says, "For best results, the counselee-helpee must really want to change, must expect that things will get better with the counselor's help, and must show a willingness to cooperate even if the counseling process is painful" (Collins 1976, 35). We need to remind ourselves that we cannot help everyone; only those who want help can cooperate in a healing relationship.

We see these two attributes at work in the persons Jesus ministered to. The hemorrhaging woman was suffering and came to Jesus because she wanted help (Mark 5:25-34). Two blind men came to Jesus because they had a physical need and wanted help (Matt. 9:27-31). Nicodemus came to Jesus because he had a felt need and wanted help (John 3:1-21).

THE COUNSELOR-COUNSELEE RELATIONSHIP

If a counselor is seeking to be effective and if the coun-

selee feels a need and wants help, it is possible for a healing relationship to develop. Marvin Mayers, while a professor of social science at Wheaton College, developed a
model for interpersonal relationships based on the concept of mutual respect. There are three basic aspects of
this model: (1) trust, (2) acceptance of self, and (3) acceptance of the other (Mayers 1974, 31-79). First we will
examine each of these three aspects and then look at the
model of mutual respect as a whole.

TRUST

A basic premise of this model is that the most effective interpersonal relationships are those which estab-
lish a bond of trust. Trust is something that develops
over the course of a relationship; it is a process as well as
an end. In order to develop a trust bond, a basic question
should always be kept in mind: "Is what I am doing,
thinking, or saying building trust or undermining trust?"
(Mayers 1974, 32) We may undermine trust without even
being aware of it because we are unaware of the verbal
and nonverbal cues or messages we are sending out. It is
important to be sensitive to behavior, as well as words,
in developing a trust bond. Gerard Egan points out that
counselors' behavior is their most important means of
communicating trustworthiness (Egan 1975, 112).

ACCEPTANCE OF SELF

In our discussion of the characteristics of effective
counselors, self-awareness is listed first. Self-awareness is foundational to the acceptance of self. However,
individuals may have a high level of self-awareness and
not accept what they are. We need to recognize that self-
acceptance is not synonymous with approval. There may
very well be aspects of one's self that need change or

further development, but "acceptance of self is the beginning point of change" (Mayers 1974, 44).

If a person has areas of weakness that fall below minimally acceptable levels or cause problems for the individual, then one needs to deal with these areas to the extent necessary for normal functioning. However, as a general rule people, including counselors, should emphasize their strengths or gifts, develop them to their fullest, and use them in their ministries. As one authority puts it:

> . . . acceptance is a major characteristic of adequate personalities. It is also a basic requirement for the helping relationship. An effective helper is one who has learned how to use himself effectively. . . . The problem of becoming effective . . . , then, is not a question of trading one's old self in for a new one. Rather, it is a matter of learning how to use the self one has and how to improve it slowly over time (Combs 1971, 298).

Acceptance of self is foundational to acceptance of others. We, as Christians, can accept ourselves because God has accepted us. He has accepted us as we are. We have worth in God's sight. God saw us as having such value that He paid for us with the life of His Son. God accepts us as we are and then works with us to bring about whatever changes are necessary.

ACCEPTANCE OF THE OTHER

As we have pointed out, acceptance of the other grows out of acceptance of self and is the essence of the trust that builds healing relationships. Acceptance of the other involves allowing the other to be himself or herself without being rejected. Again acceptance does not mean approval. In the counseling situation, others come to us because they realize there is a problem, that something needs to be done. But, as with self-acceptance, acceptance of the other is the beginning point for change. When we accept others they become more self-aware and can more accurately evaluate themselves and their situation. This, in turn, becomes the basis for real change. As Mayers says, "Complete openness in acceptance will encourage the other also to be completely open; thus openness provides the fertile soil for change" (Mayers 1974, 66).

Christian counselors are in a position to accept others because they have been accepted by God and the other has been accepted by God. As Mayers says,

> The acceptance of the other person deals with the acceptance-rejection patterns underlying interpersonal relationships. Rejection produces alienation; acceptance reverses alienation and is the sound foundation for true Christian love ... for the Gospel would reverse the process of rejection and insure acceptance (Mayers 1974, 66).

MODEL OF MUTUAL RESPECT

Mayers's model of mutual respect, as well as the characteristics of effective counselors, can be related to Carl Rogers's* list of ten characteristics of a helping relationship (Rogers 1961, 50-56).

1.   *Can I be in some way which will be perceived by the other person as trustworthy, as dependable or consistent in some deep sense?*

This relates to both trustworthiness and genuineness. It is important that others perceive our trustworthiness.

---

*Carl Rogers is sometimes misinterpreted and falsely slandered by some evangelical writers. Rogers does not write from an evangelical perspective and while we do not accept all that he says, we can learn from him. All truth is God's truth, even if it is discovered or reported by someone who does not view Christianity as we do.

This is critical for building a trust relationship.

2. Can I be expressive enough as a person that what I am will be communicated unambiguously?

If we want our counselees to be genuine or open with us we need to be genuine and open with them. The counseling relationship is not the place for putting on an act. We need to be ourselves in order to develop a true trust relationship.

3. Can I let myself experience positive attitudes toward this other person—attitudes of warmth, caring, liking, interest, respect?

This point relates to the concept of acceptance of the other and the characteristic of warmth. In order to express warmth for others we need to feel such warmth. Acceptance of others is the key to feeling warmth for others. As Christians, we are indwelt with the love of Christ which empowers us to accept others and feel warmth toward them.

4. Can I be strong enough as a person to be separate from the other? Can I be a sturdy respector of my own feelings, my own needs, as well as his? Can I own and, if need be, express my own feelings as something belonging to me and separate from his feelings?

This characteristic relates both to self-awareness and self-acceptance. Acceptance of others does not mean we deny either ourselves or our values. We need to be aware of who we are and what we believe. It is only when we know and accept ourselves and our beliefs that we are truly free to accept others. We can accept those who differ from us without covering up who we are. Jesus was able to accept publicans and sinners without denying who He was or compromising His message.

5. Am I secure enough within myself to permit him his separateness? Can I permit him to be what he is . . .?

This concern builds directly on the previous point. When we are secure in ourselves we can allow others to be themselves. When we are not secure in ourselves, others tend to be a threat to us so we either reject them or deny who they are. As Christians our security lies in the fact that God has accepted us in Christ Jesus. Because God has accepted us we can be secure enough to accept others.

6. *Can I let myself enter fully into the world of his feelings and personal meanings and see these as he does?*

This is the concept of empathy, the ability to put ourselves in someone else's shoes. It is only when we begin to see things from other persons' perspectives that we will truly be able to help them. This is what Paul means when he says, *Rejoice with those who rejoice; mourn with those who mourn* (Rom. 12:15).

7. *Can I receive him as he is? Can I communicate this attitude?*

Accepting others is of little value if we do not communicate this acceptance. It is through warmth and empathy that we communicate acceptance to others.

8. *Can I act with sufficient sensitivity in the relationship that my behavior will not be perceived as a threat?*

This point relates to the basic question raised earlier, "Is what I am doing, thinking, or saying building trust or undermining it?" We need to be sensitive to our behavior and monitor it to be certain we are communicating what we want to communicate. We may feel warmth and empathy, but does the other feel it?

9. *Can I free him from the threat of external evaluation?*

This is the essence of a trust relationship where true acceptance of others is present. This does not imply a lack of evaluation, but rather that evaluation must begin within the other. We need to accept others in order to free them to evaluate themselves and their situations. It is out of this self-evaluation that real change will come. The Word of God gives us a basis on which true evaluation can be made. It may be appropriate for us to share relevant Scriptures with others to aid them in the process of self-evaluation.

10.   Can I meet this other individual as a person who is in the process of becoming . . . ?

It might be good if all of us wore signs that read, "Please be patient with me, God is not finished with me yet." Maybe the most important point in this whole chapter is that acceptance is the beginning point for change. It is only as we accept others as persons in the process of becoming what they can be, that we can help them on the way.

Mutual respect in the counseling process is based on all ten of these characteristics. It is the foundation for healing relationships. However, counseling involves more than a relationship, it also involves content, an aspect which will be covered in the next chapter.

DISCUSSION QUESTIONS

1.   *Which of the effective counselor characteristics are most developed in your life? least developed?*
2.   *How much help can you give to a person who does not feel he needs help? Why do you feel that way?*
3.   *Is it possible to accept a person who is doing something you disapprove of? Why?*
4.   *Why is the relationship between the counselor and counselee the major key to counseling effectiveness?*
5.   *Why is acceptance the beginning point of change?*

SUGGESTED READING

Combs, Arthur W., et al. *Helping Relationships.* Boston: Allyn and Bacon, 1971. A secular text written from a humanistic perspective. While the reader will want to be discriminating, there are some very helpful discussions in this work, particularly on self-acceptance.

Mallory, James D., Jr. *The Kink and I.* Wheaton: Victor Books, 1973. A helpful book in the areas of self-awareness and self-acceptance. Written by a Christian psychiatrist.

McGinnis, Alan Loy. *The Friendship Factor.* Minneapolis: Augsburg, 1979. One of the better books on the popular market considering interpersonal relationships. Written by a Christian psychologist, this book should be *must* reading for anyone seriously interested in lay counseling.

CHAPTER FOUR

Theory for Lay Counseling: Responsibility

The story is told of a young man who was on trial for the murder of his mother and father. The defense lawyer, in making his summation to the jury, said, "In considering my client's guilt or innocence please consider his background, after all he is an orphan." While we find this story amusing, it raises an important question: are individuals generally responsible for their behavior?

The content of the counseling process must be based on the concept of responsibility. The discussion of the essence of human nature in chapter 2 indicated that one aspect of the image of God in humans is rationality and that rationality is related to responsibility. Because humans have the ability to reason and their behavior is subject to their reason (e.g., 2 Cor. 8:11; 10:5), humans are responsible for their behavior (e.g., Matt. 12:35-37). This truth is illustrated in Jesus' parable of the talents where one servant buried his talent and then returned it. The servant was held responsible for his action because he was capable of knowing his master wanted a return on the investment and he knew how to obtain it. The servant was held responsible because he was a rational being (Matt. 25:14-30; Luke 19:11-26).

An understanding of the biblical concept of "heart" is helpful in understanding humans as rational and responsible beings. The Hebrew word for "heart" is *lebab* or *leb*; the Greek word is *kardia*. In their literal sense, both the Hebrew and Greek words mean the same as the English word. They refer to the large muscle located in the chest which pumps blood throughout the body. However, in Scripture, as in English, the word *heart* is often used in a figurative sense. In English the heart is symbolic of romance and emotions. At times there is almost an irrational quality attached to it as in the expression, "He was led by his heart instead of his head."

The heart, in Scripture, is symbolic of at least three human functions (Kittel 1967, 3:606-13). First, the heart, in both the Old and New Testaments, is seen as the seat of rational functions or reasoning (e.g., Deut. 29:4, AV; 1 Kings 3:12; Job 37:24; Prov. 2:2; 14:33; Luke 2:51; 24:38, AV; Acts 8:22; Heb. 4:12). Second, the heart symbolizes decision making or the will (e.g., 1 Kings 8:17; Prov. 16:9; Isa. 10:7, AV; Jer. 23:20; Mark 7:21; Acts 5:3; 1 Cor. 4:5; 2 Cor. 9:7). Third, the heart symbolizes the spiritual essence of humans, that aspect of human nature that is capable of responding to God (e.g., 1 Sam. 12:20, 24; Prov. 7:3; Isa. 51:7; Jer. 32:40, AV; Luke 16:15; Rom. 8:27; 1 Thess. 2:4). These three functions of the heart are interrelated. The heart symbolizes much of the image of God in humans. Because humans are rational, reasoning beings, they choose their behavior. Because humans choose their behavior they are responsible for that behavior. Any approach to counseling, to be consistent with the biblical view of humanity, must treat humans as beings responsible to God.

APPROACHES TO COUNSELING

We may divide the theoretical approaches to counseling into four major schools: psychodynamic, behavioral, humanistic, and cognitive. The *psychodynamic* school has its roots in the work of Sigmund Freud. While most counselors in this school have moved beyond Freud and have modified many of his emphases, a common factor is the focus on the dynamic interaction between the unconscious and the conscious. This position sees both human behavior and problems rooted in the unconscious or subconscious. A major contribution of the psychodynamic approach is that it has made people aware that many mental processes, such as defense mechanisms, operate on an unconscious level. This school's major problem is its tendency toward instinctive determinism, that is, seeing human behavior as controlled by drives and instincts, thereby minimizing personal responsibility.

The *behavioral* school has its roots in the work of people like William Watson and B. F. Skinner. This approach is not as concerned with mental processes as it is with behavior. The approach is based on the principle that behavior which is rewarded will continue or increase while behavior that is punished will decrease or disappear. Therefore, desirable behaviors should be rewarded while problematic or undesirable behaviors should be punished. This approach to therapy has had some success in dealing with problems such as smoking, drugs, and homosexuality. Its shortcoming is that it treats humans as mechanisms and sees external factors as determining an individual's behavior. It allows no room for personal responsibility.*

The *humanistic* school, for the most part, has had its roots in the psychodynamic school. It also has certain

---

*We need to distinguish between the techniques of behaviorism which are often quite helpful and the philosophy of behaviorism which treats humans as machines and strips humanity of its soul.

perspectives in common with the cognitive school. It has grown out of the work of people such as Carl Rogers, Rollo May, Viktor Frankl, and Abraham Maslow. This approach began as a reaction against the instinctive determinism of the psychodynamic school and the mechanistic determinism of the behavioral school. This view sees humans as responsible beings who determine their own behavior (at least within social and ecological limits). The humanistic approach is concerned with the dignity and worth of individuals and seeks to work with them to develop their fullest potential. One of its major contributions has been an emphasis on the uniqueness of humanity, on humans' ability to choose their own behavior, and on human responsibility. A major problem is that if carried to a logical conclusion, it ultimately sets humankind up as its own god. Another problem is the view of human nature. The tendency is to see human nature as good, or at worst, neutral. This is contrary to the doctrine of the Fall and the consequences of sin.

While each of these perspectives has both theoretical and methodological contributions to make to an approach to counseling, the perspective that seems most consistent with the theology of counseling developed in chapter 2 is the *cognitive* school. This school of thought emphasizes cognitive and rational processes as well as emotions. The cognitive approach treats persons as rational and responsible. Such people as Albert Ellis, O. Hobart Mowrer, Aaron Beck, and William Glasser have made major contributions to this perspective. Within the cognitive school there are variations in the approaches of each theorist. Of these cognitive approaches, Glasser's Reality Therapy* seems to be particularly adaptable to a Christian perspective. Quentin Hyder, a Christian

---

*While Glasser calls his approach a "therapy," in many respects it fits the definition of "counseling" better.

psychiatrist, points out that Reality Therapy lends itself to integration with a biblical perspective (Hyder 1971, 167-76).

REALITY THERAPY

There are three aspects of Reality Therapy that make it readily adaptable to Christian lay counseling. First, as Glasser points out, Reality Therapy lends itself to use by nonprofessionals or lay counselors (Glasser 1965, 27-28). Second, Reality Therapy builds heavily on the counselor-counselee relationship. Glasser sees the characteristics of the counselor as central to this relationship. He particularly emphasizes the characteristics of warmth, understanding, and acceptance. Third, Reality Therapy calls for moral responsibility. It needs to be pointed out that Glasser does not offer a standard of right and wrong, but rather expects people to live up to their own or society's standards. However, his call for moral responsibility is consistent with the biblical view of human nature. The Christian counselor has the Bible to evaluate the standards of individuals and critique the standards of society.

Glasser sees most personal problems arising from individuals' inability to meet their basic needs. Unsuccessful attempts to meet these needs result from a denial of some or all of the reality of the surrounding world. This is often just an evasion of responsibility. Lawrence Crabb, a Christian psychologist who also finds the cognitive approach compatible with the scriptural view of humanity, points out that people make choices based on what they believe is true (Crabb 1977, 100-101). Therefore, if a person's beliefs are false or unrealistic the decisions based on those beliefs are likely to be unrealistic as well. Individuals can meet their needs successfully only if they deal with them realistically.

Glasser says humans have two primary psychological needs (Glasser 1965, 9-10). The first is the need to love and be loved. We know that we are capable of loving and being loved because we are made in the image of God who is love. We should note that the New Testament speaks of love as an act of the will rather than an emotion. It is an action not a feeling. The Scriptures command love. It is treated as something one can will to do (e.g., Matt. 22:37-40; John 13:34-35; 15:17; 1 John 3:23).

Viktor Frankl, a psychotherapist who complements Glasser's position on love, argues that real love is spiritual in nature. It is basically not an emotion but rather an act of the will. Frankl says, " . . . the meaningfulness of human existence is based upon the uniqueness and singularity of the human person. . . . Love is living the experience of another person in all his uniqueness and singularity." He adds, "In love the beloved person is comprehended in his very essence, as the unique and singular being that he is; he is comprehended as a Thou, and as such is taken into the self" (Frankl 1965, 136-37). God has made us so that we need a loving relationship with other humans and ultimately with Him in order to be whole.

The second of Glasser's primary psychological needs is to feel worthwhile both to oneself and to others. He goes on to say that feeling worthwhile results from behaving responsibly. Glasser says, "Morals, standards, values, or right and wrong behavior are all intimately related to the fulfillment of our need for self-worth. . . ." He also says, "If we do not evaluate our own behavior, or having evaluated it, we do not act to improve our conduct where it is below our standards, we will not fulfill our need to be worthwhile . . ." (Glasser 1965, 10-11). Frankl, agreeing with Glasser, says, " . . . being human means being conscious and being responsible." To what then are we, as humans, responsible, up to what standard do we need to live? Frankl goes beyond Glasser and answers,

> ... the self cannot be responsible merely to itself. The self cannot be its own lawgiver. It can never issue any autonomous 'categorical imperative,' for a categorical imperative can receive its credentials only from transcendence. Its categorical character stands and falls with its transcendent quality. It is true that man is responsible for himself. Not only man's being free, but also his being responsible requires an intentional referent. Just as freedom means little, indeed means nothing, without a 'to what,' likewise responsibleness is incomplete without a 'to what' (Frankl 1975, 57).

To "what" are we responsible? We are responsible to God our Creator. It is only in God that we ultimately find self-worth. Part of the reality that we need to face is our need to be properly related to God through Jesus Christ.

While Reality Therapy recognizes the place of emotions in human personality and behavior, its approach is consistent with recent psychological research which indicates that emotions are more a by-product of thought and behavior than a cause (Braun and Kinder 1979, 337-56). In Scripture human behavior is generally attributed to the heart—the center of rationality, the will, and responsibility—rather than to emotions which are seen as centered in the bowels. While there are circumstances when one should legitimately experience emotions, the resolution of these emotions involves cognitive processes and behavioral action.

We need to be careful in counseling not to ignore emotions. Emotions are often a key to understanding problems. Individuals may claim something does not upset them, but their emotions may indicate otherwise. They cannot successfully deal with their emotions if they deny the underlying reality. The fact that feelings are a result of thinking and action, rather than a cause, does not make them any less important. The Scriptures teach that we are to respond to people's emotions (Rom. 12:15).

It is important for us to realize that emotions will always be expressed. They may be talked out and worked out. They may be acted out in irresponsible, deviant, or abnormal behavior. They may break out in physical illness such as ulcers (see chapter 9, for a discussion of psychosomatic illness). People's emotions will come out and we best serve our counselees, not by ignoring or downplaying their emotions, but by helping them to express their emotions in healthy ways.

DEFENSE MECHANISMS

One of the ways in which people attempt to handle their problems is through the use of what are called defense mechanisms. Reality can be threatening and unpleasant. People sometimes find it easier to avoid reality than to deal with it. Defense mechanisms are one way people avoid reality. These defense mechanisms generally operate on an unconscious level to deny or distort some aspect of reality. In fact, all defense mechanisms are, at least to some degree, a form of self-deception. While all of us utilize these defense mechanisms at one time or another, excessive use of these defense mechanisms is unhealthy and dysfunctional.

There are at least six commonly used defense mechanisms. The first of these mechanisms is *rationalization*. Rationalization involves telling ourselves, or others, that a situation is not what it seems. For example, a man who is turned down for a job may rationalize that he was overqualified or too good for the job. A student who is not accepted by the college of her choice suddenly discovers a number of reasons why she would not be happy at that college anyway. Parents may not want to see their children grow up and leave home so they become overly protective of them and rationalize that they are being good parents. The problem with rationalizing is that it does not allow people to accept themselves and change. As long as he rationalizes, the man who was turned down for the job will not be able to work on the issues that kept him from getting the job.

The second defense mechanism is *repression*. Repression involves pushing problematic aspects of reality from one's mind. For example, a son might be angry with his father. Since hating one's father is not socially acceptable, the boy represses his anger and convinces himself he is not angry. This defense mechanism is often utilized by Christians. Since they are not supposed to hate others or be angry with others, there is a tendency to repress these feelings. The problem is that repression does not make something go away, it only pushes it into the subconscious where it can lead to physical problems such as ulcers, emotional problems such as anxiety or depression, or behavioral problems such as antisocial behavior. The way to deal with hate or anger or any other issue is not to repress it but face it. What has made one angry or hateful? When the issue is faced it can be dealt with rationally and responsibly.

The third defense mechanism is *displacement*. This mechanism involves displacing or shifting a reaction from one object onto another. For example, a man may feel like lashing out at his boss, but is afraid of the consequences, so he goes home and yells at his wife. People often use displacement when they are unable to express their feelings toward a particular person, so they displace those feelings onto someone to whom they can express themselves. Again, reality is denied and rather than solving a problem, new problems are often created. By displacing his anger, the man who is mad at his boss has not only not solved that problem but has also created a new one with his wife.

The fourth defense mechanism is *projection*. This mechanism involves the attribution of one's motives and thoughts onto others. For example, if a person is tempted to be dishonest in a certain situation he assumes everyone else would be similarly tempted. A jealous husband may accuse his wife of being jealous. Many people think others dislike them, when in reality they are only projecting their dislike for themselves. Psychologists generally recognize this as the most powerful of all the defense mechanisms. People usually project weaknesses and problems. Projection has the potential for destroying relationships by distorting reality.

The fifth defense mechanism is *reaction formation*. This mechanism involves substituting an unacceptable feeling or motive with its opposite. A father may feel resentment toward a child, but unconsciously realizes it is wrong for a father to react that way, so he showers the child with expressions of love and material things such as toys. A woman might want a dominant position in a relationship but unconsciously feels that is unfeminine, so she reacts by acting overly helpless. The person who fights the hardest against pornography may have the greatest temptation for it.

The sixth defense mechanism is *denial*. This involves completely denying, or not accepting, reality. Denial is often used when we are suddenly faced with an aspect of reality that overwhelms us. For example, most persons practice denial when confronted with the sudden death of a loved one. A woman who is told her husband has just been killed in an automobile accident may respond, "It couldn't be him, it must be a mistake." Denial in such instances is a healthy response. It allows the individual an opportunity to adjust to reality. This defense mechanism becomes a problem when it continues too long and the person does not adjust to reality. When denial becomes a fixed response to reality, the person needs professional help.

Each of these defense mechanisms, in some way, denies or distorts reality. We need to be aware of these defense mechanisms in order to help our counselees face reality, instead of trying to escape from responsibility. When people face reality and accept responsibility, change can take place. We should remember that these defense mechanisms are unconscious. Individuals are not consciously aware they are using them. We should not try to break through a person's defense mechanisms. In some cases this may result in a psychotic reaction, a severe psychological condition where a person loses complete touch with reality. We should help counselees dismantle their defense mechanisms themselves as they move toward reality.

Reality Therapy is a counseling approach that recognizes that personal problems generally arise from unsuccessful attempts to meet one's needs. Successful attempts to meet one's needs involve dealing with reality in a responsible manner. We need to build healing relationships with our counselees so we may work together to deal with reality in a responsible way. The counselee, with our help, determines a responsible course of action for resolving the problem and carries it out, reporting the results to us. The results are evaluated and appropriate adjustments, if necessary, may be made. The Christian counselor, with the counselee, looks to Scripture for guidelines to responsible behavior.

APPLYING REALITY THERAPY

A basic concept of Reality Therapy is that most people's problems result from a refusal to accept responsibility for behavior. Therefore, counseling involves helping people evaluate their behavior realistically. They need to see clearly what is causing the problem. Next, counseling involves getting people to accept responsibility for their behavior. Finally, counseling involves helping people think through behavioral changes to solve their problems.

William Glasser has set forth seven basic principles or steps for applying Reality Therapy in counseling (Glasser 1972, 107-32). The first principle is that counseling begins with *involvement*. The counselor must be willing to become involved with the counselee. The healing relationship between counselor and counselee is the key to the remaining principles. The second principle or step is that the *current behavior* of the counselee should be examined. People often avoid examining their behavior by focusing on their feelings. While feelings are important, we need to get behind the feelings to the behavior and/or thinking that is causing the feelings. Examining emotions alone is a dead-end street. Determining the behavior that is causing the distress leads to the next step.

The third principle is that the counselee must *evaluate* his or her *behavior* in a rational manner and decide that his or her behavior is causing the problem. Many problems people face do have causes outside themselves. However, the only solutions that they control are their responses to these outside causes. While people may not be able to change situations they can change these responses. For example, in the case of the death of a loved one, people cannot change the death. However, they can change their thinking and behavior in response to that death. For Christians the Bible is the primary basis for the evaluation of behavior. We should not hesitate to use appropriate Scripture at this step.

The fourth principle is that the counselee should be assisted in planning *responsible behavior*. The counselee needs to have an active part in this. We need to avoid the temptation to impose a plan. We should insist that whatever plan the counselee develops, it is realistic, that it does not avoid reality. That means when a counselee makes an unrealistic suggestion we need to remind the counselee of reality. Rather than telling the counselee that the suggestion is unrealistic, it is better to help the counselee discover it. This can often be done by asking questions pointed toward the unrealistic aspect of the suggestion such as, "Where will you get the money for that?" or "Do you have time for that?" or "How do you think so-and-so will react when you do that?" Again, for Christians the Bible is a source of principles to guide the development of a plan of action. Also it is important to pray for God's guidance in developing the plan.

One other important point that Glasser makes about this step is that one should never make a plan of action that attempts too much. If the plan fails it will merely reinforce the existing problem. People need to experience success to overcome their problems. It is better to develop a plan consisting of a series of small, easily attainable steps than a complex plan that might fail. All of a person's problems cannot be solved in one step.

The fifth principle or step is that the counselee make a *commitment* to the plan. After a reasonable plan of action has been developed, it needs to be carried out. As Christians, prayer should be part of the verbal commitment process. The Christian does not carry out the plan of action alone. The believer is indwelt by the Holy Spirit and needs to seek His power and wisdom.

We would like to add a subpoint to this point. Steps two through five may need to be repeated. What may have seemed a realistic plan of action in the counseling session may not prove to be realistic in practice because of elements that were not considered when the plan was made or unforeseen changes in the situation. Counselor and counselee should not become slavishly locked into a plan. They need to be flexible and monitor the plan as they go, making needed corrections as necessary.

The sixth principle is that the counselor should *accept no excuses*. If a plan is realistic and the situation has not changed it should be carried out. Excuses just reinforce failure. The person has made a commitment. If it is realistic the counselor should hold the counselee to it. If the plan turns out to be unrealistic, revise it and have a new commitment. Responsibility involves accountability. Lay counselors can hold counselees accountable by refusing to sympathize with irresponsibility and by encouraging the person to follow the agreed-upon plan.

The seventh principle is that the counselor should give *no punishment*. When a person has lived up to a commitment, praise is in order. Praise leads to responsible behavior, it reinforces success. Affirmation is an important counseling tool. If a person fails he or she needs support, not punishment. However, excuses are not accepted and the person who fails starts the process over again.

The key to this approach to counseling is responsibility. People need to take responsibility for their behavior if they are going to solve their problems.* This approach is consistent with our understanding of the biblical view of human nature.

---

*While cognition and behavior have been stressed in this approach, it is important for counselors to remember that humans also have a physical nature and that there may be physical causes for problematic behavior. A counselor should inquire about physical problems and ask the counselee if he or she is on drugs (prescription as well as nonprescription). A ready source for ascertaining the side effects of drugs is the *Physicians' Desk Reference*, 34th ed. (Oradell, N.J.: Medical Economics, Inc., 1980).

DISCUSSION QUESTIONS

1. What role does a person's heredity and environment play in his behavior? How does this affect individual responsibility?
2. Do you believe Christians can learn from scholars with non-Christian assumptions? Why?
3. Why is the counselor-counselee relationship the first and basic principle in Glasser's approach?
4. Why do people often focus on their feelings rather than their behavior?
5. Do you apply the Reality Therapy approach to problems in your life?

SUGGESTED READING

Basin, Alexander, Bratter, Thomas, and Rachin, Richard, eds. *The Reality Therapy Reader.* New York: Harper & Row, 1976. A collection of articles by Glasser and other Reality Therapists explaining the theory and its practice.

Collins, Gary. *The Rebuilding of Psychology.* Wheaton: Tyndale, 1977. A good critique of various schools of psychology from a Christian perspective.

Cosgrove, Mark. *Psychology Gone Awry.* Grand Rapids: Zondervan, 1979. Another critique of various schools of psychology from a Christian perspective.

Crabb, Lawrence J., Jr. *Effective Biblical Counseling.* Grand Rapids: Zondervan, 1977. A work presenting a model or theory of counseling based on a cognitive perspective. The model treats individuals as rational and responsible beings who have basic needs. It views most problems as arising from unrealistic or irresponsible behavioral attempts to meet those needs. It suggests biblical patterns for meeting needs.

Glasser, William. *Reality Therapy.* New York: Harper &

Row, 1965. Glasser's original work on his theory. Explains the theory and contains case studies demonstrating its use.

_____. *The Identity Society*. New York: Harper & Row, 1972. Contains Glasser's discussion of the seven principles of Reality Therapy.

CHAPTER FIVE

Theory for Lay Counseling: Religion

Two women who had marital problems were talking over lunch at a local restaurant. One of the women explained how she was seeing a professional marriage counselor. The other woman confided she was seeing her pastor about her problems. The two women began comparing the counsel they were receiving.

What is it that distinguishes Christian counseling from secular counseling? Wayne Oates, a seminary professor of pastoral counseling, points out that while Christian counseling is similar to secular counseling in many respects, there are several important distinctives. These distinctives are religious* in nature (Oates 1974, 11-25). The first one he lists is that the Christian counselor recognizes God's existence in the reality the counselor and counselee work with. This reality involves the Christian counselor being in a right relation with God. Also, Christian counselees need to be in a right relationship with God. It is the counselor's and counselee's

---

*When we use the terms *religion* and *religious*, we are referring to the spiritual dimension of faith rather than the organizational dimension.

relationship to God that makes counseling uniquely Christian.

The second distinctive is that the relationship with God affects the counseling process. If God makes a difference in our life, He will make a difference in our counseling. Even when counseling with a non-Christian, who is not interested in spiritual things, our faith should make itself felt without forcing it on the counselee.

Another distinctive of Christian counseling is that it draws on the resources of Scripture. The place of Scripture in counseling will be discussed later in this chapter. A fourth distinctive is that Christian counseling uses the resources of the Christian community, the church. Christian counseling is not meant to be a "lone ranger" operation. The full resources of the church—spiritual, social, and physical—should be used as needed.

An additional distinctive of Christian counseling, suggests Oates, is the place of ethics in counseling. While a secular counselor may practice ethical relativity, the Christian counselor's approach is grounded in Christian ethics. These ethical considerations include confidentiality, proper relations with members of the opposite sex, the welfare of the counselee, and a biblical morality.

RESOURCES

We see at least three basic resources of the Christian religion that need to be utilized by Christian counselors. They are (1) the Holy Spirit, (2) the Bible, and (3) prayer. All three of these resources need to be used by the effective counselor. We will examine each of these resources in more detail.

THE HOLY SPIRIT

Evangelical Christians believe the Holy Spirit is the

third member of the Trinity. The Holy Spirit is a person or personality rather than just a force or principle. God has revealed Himself in three persons, the Father, the Son, and the Holy Spirit. The Holy Spirit is a person in the same way the Father and the Son are persons. Scripture indicates that each person of the Godhead has a distinctive function, His own work to accomplish. The Holy Spirit has specific functions that are relevant to the ministry of counseling.

One of the functions of the Holy Spirit involves reconciling people to God. As has been pointed out, counseling can never be fully effective until the counselee is reconciled to God.* The New Testament indicates at least two aspects of the Holy Spirit's ministry in the reconciliation process. The first is convicting individuals of sin (John 16:7-11). It is sin, human rebellion against God, that damaged their relationship to God and this rebellion needs to be recognized and dealt with for reconciliation to take place (1 John 1:8-10). Second, it is the Holy Spirit who regenerates, or gives new life to, the one who comes to God through Jesus Christ (John 3:5-8; Rom. 8:1-2; Titus 3:5). We need to recognize and utilize the reconciling work of the Holy Spirit in counseling.

Another function of the Holy Spirit is giving insight into, or understanding of, the Scriptures (John 16:13; 1 Cor. 2:9-10; 1 John 2:20, 27). The Bible is one of the religious resources upon which we draw. As we use Scripture for our own instruction or to minister to others, the Holy Spirit helps us to understand and apply it.

An additional function of the Holy Spirit is to come

---

*This does not mean that Christian counselors cannot counsel with or help those who are not reconciled to God. However, apart from reconciliation to God, that person can never reach his or her full potential and help will be limited.

alongside believers to help them. In John 14:16, 26; 15:26; and 16:7, Jesus called the Holy Spirit the *parakletos*. This word is translated "comforter" in the Authorized Version and "counselor" in the Revised Standard Version and the New International Version. Other translators prefer "supporter" or "helper" (Kittel 1967, 5:814). This support or help from the Holy Spirit, for believers, takes two forms according to Jesus' teaching as recorded in John's Gospel. The first is to teach, a continuation of the teaching ministry of Jesus (John 14:16-26; 15:26). The second is to guide believers (John 16:13). The Holy Spirit as a teacher and guide is available to us as well as our Christian counselees. We need to be filled with the Holy Spirit (Eph. 5:18) and to walk in the Spirit (Gal. 5:16). Basically, this means to be yielded to the Holy Spirit, to be attentive and obedient to His teaching, and to follow His guidance. Christian counselees also have the Holy Spirit available to them. We need to work with our counselees in allowing the Holy Spirit to guide and direct as they formulate a plan of action. It should be noted that the processes used by the Holy Spirit—teaching and guiding—are rational and cognitive processes. The Holy Spirit helps the believer think correctly and therefore behave correctly (Rom. 8:5-11). Christian counseling, to be effective, must rely on the ministry of the Holy Spirit in both the counselor and the counselee.

An additional ministry of the Holy Spirit involves the development of character traits such as love, joy, peace, patience, kindness, goodness, faithfulness, gentleness, and self-control (Gal. 5:22-23; Rom. 14:17). Christian counseling does not depend solely on natural processes but also on the supernatural enablement; this is why reconciliation to God is such an important aspect of Christian counseling: it allows supernatural enablement.

THE BIBLE

One of the most important resources of the Christian counselor is the Bible. Waylon Ward suggests there are six uses of the Bible in counseling (Ward 1977, 17-18). One of these uses is *confrontation*. Ward admits that this use of the Bible is being abused in some counseling circles today. However, he goes on to point out that just because some have misused the Bible in this way does not mean there is not a legitimate role for the Scriptures in confrontation. Confrontation does not involve attacking or blaming but focuses on that behavior in need of modification. The New Testament teaches that Scripture is to be used for correction (e.g., 2 Tim. 3:16; 4:2; Heb. 4:12). While confrontation should always be done in love (Eph. 4:15) and gentleness (2 Tim. 2:25), there are times when we must confront a counselee with the teachings of Scripture.

Second, the Bible should be used for *teaching* (e.g., Titus 1:9; 2 Tim. 3:16). The Bible addresses every area of human life. The Bible, for example, speaks specifically about the relationships between husband and wife, parent and child, employer and employee, person and person (e.g., Eph. 5:21—6:9). The Bible talks about attitudes and behavior. The Bible talks about birth and death and all that comes between. We should be as knowledgeable as possible about the Scriptures so that we can draw upon the teachings of the Bible as they apply to the counseling situation.

The third use of the Bible in counseling is *meditation* (e.g., Ps. 1:2; Phil. 1:8; 2 Cor. 10:5). Wayne Oates sees Bible meditation as a source of inner strength (Oates 1953, 101), while William Hulme suggests that counselors assign relevant passages of Scripture for counselees to meditate on as homework (Hulme 1956, 207-10). A list of Scripture passages related to various problems is presented in Table 5-1.

Fourth, the Bible may be a source of *comfort* (e.g., 2 Cor. 1:3-4; 1 Thess. 4:18). Oates has devoted a whole chapter in his book on the Bible in counseling to this subject. In that chapter he discusses appropriate Scripture passages for various situations. The more we know about biblical principles and how they were worked out in the lives of Bible characters the more we will be able to help our counselees.

Fifth, counselors should use the Bible *as a source of ethical principles for behavior*. It has been pointed out that Reality Therapy calls for moral responsibility but does not offer an ethical standard to which one can be responsible. For the Christian, the Bible provides this ethical standard. Humans are beings responsible to God, and His standards are set forth in the Bible. Many of the verses in Psalm 119 focus on this aspect of God's Word (e.g., vv. 9-11, 133, 138).

The last use of the Bible in counseling suggested by Ward is *as a means of changing behavior*. The Bible calls for obedience to its teachings (e.g., John 14:15, 21; 15:10; Phil. 4:9; James 1:25; Rev. 1:3). As the counselor and counselee work together to develop a plan of action, they need to do so in the light of Scripture. The Bible should have a central role in Christian counseling.

PRAYER

Prayer has at least two applications in Christian counseling. First, we need to *pray for ourselves*. The counselor needs to pray for wisdom, strength, and guidance before meeting with counselees. We do not enter the counseling situation alone; in the person of the Holy Spirit, God is also present. We should seek the help of God to carry out our ministries. We realize we are doing God's work and need His help.

TABLE 5-1

SCRIPTURE PASSAGES FOR USE IN COUNSELING

PROBLEM OR NEED	PASSAGES
Anxiety or Worry	Psalm 43:5; 46:1-11; Proverbs 3:5-6; Matthew 6:31-32; John 14:26-27; Romans 8:38-39; Philippians 4:6-7, 19; 1 Peter 5:6-7.
Anger	Psalm 37:8; Ephesians 4:26-27; Colossians 3:8; James 1:19.
Bereavement and Loss	Deuteronomy 31:8; Psalm 27:10; 119:50, 92; 2 Corinthians 6:10; Philippians 3:8.
Comfort	Matthew 11:28-30; 2 Corinthians 1:3-4; 2 Thessalonians 2:16-17.
Confidence	Psalm 27:3; Proverbs 3:26; 14:26; Isaiah 30:15; Ephesians 3:11-12; Philippians 4:13.
Death	Psalm 23; John 14:1-6; 1 Corinthians 15:1-58; 1 Thessalonians 5:9-10.
Discouragement	Joshua 1:9; Psalm 27:14; 43:5; John 14:1-27; 16:33; Hebrews 4:16; 1 John 5:14.
Envy	Psalm 37:1-7; Proverbs 23:17; Romans 13:13; Galatians 5:26.

Forgiving Others	*Matthew 5:44-47; 6:12-14; Ephesians 4:32; Colossians 3:13.*
Frustration	*Psalm 37:4; 73:1-28.*
Guidance	*Psalm 32:8; Proverbs 3:5-6; John 16:13.*
Guilt	*Psalm 32:5; 51:1-19; Proverbs 28:13; Isaiah 1:18; 55:7; James 5:15-16; 1 John 1:9; 2:1-2.*
Hatred	*Ephesians 4:31-32; 1 John 2:9-11.*
Helplessness	*Psalm 34:7; 37:5, 24; 55:22; 91:4; Hebrews 4:16; 13:5-6; 1 Peter 5:7.*
Loneliness	*Psalm 27:10; Proverbs 18:24; Isaiah 41:10; Matthew 28:20; John 15:14; Hebrews 13:5.*
Patience	*Galatians 5:22; Hebrews 10:36; James 1:3-4; 5:7-8, 11.*
Peace	*Isaiah 26:3; John 14:27; 16:33; Romans 5:1; Philippians 4:7; Colossians 3:15.*
Salvation	*John 1:12; 3:16; Acts 4:12; Romans 3:23; 6:23; 10:9-10; Ephesians 2:8-10.*
Sickness	*Psalm 41:3; 103:3; James 5:14-15.*
Temptation	*1 Corinthians 10:12-13; 2 Timothy 2:22; Hebrews 2:18; James 1:2-4, 12; 2 Peter 2:9.*
Wisdom	*Proverbs 2:1-11; 4:7; James 1:5.*

Second, *prayer* can be a powerful resource *in the counseling situation.* However, prayer may be misused. William Hulme points out that prayer should not be something "tacked on" the end of a session nor should it be used to make a session "spiritual," rather prayer should be used, when appropriate, as an integral part of the counseling process (Hulme 1970, 156-58).

In counseling, prayer may be used for confession in dealing with real guilt. Prayer may be used to ask guidance in developing a course of action. Prayer may be used to make a commitment. Prayer may be used to seek healing, both physical and psychological. We need to make the wise use of prayer an important part of our counseling approach.

While we have available the resources of our religion—the Holy Spirit, the Bible, and prayer—we need to use these resources wisely. As Collins points out,

The spiritual can be introduced too quickly and too abruptly. Some helpees have been turned off in the past by well-meaning but pushy Christians who have rushed in to present the gospel or to give mini-sermons on how to live better lives. The helper must be sensitive to the Holy Spirit's leading, at times not even mentioning spiritual things at all (Collins 1976, 55).

We must be sensitive to the needs and feelings of the counselee as well as to the leading of the Holy Spirit in introducing the spiritual dimension. On the other hand we should not suppress the spiritual. It is the spiritual dimension that makes Christian counseling Christian.

While we should not force our religious convictions on a counselee, even as God does not force Himself on us, we should offer the resources of our faith to the counselee. We can bear witness to what God has done in our lives. Because grace has been extended to us by God, we are able to extend grace to the counselee. As Len Sperry, a marriage and family counselor, says, "A Christian believes that a person can love only because he has been loved first, that he can relate intimately to another only because he is born out of the inner intimacy of God Himself." He goes on to say, "Just as all of us need to be affirmed by another to grow, the Christian finds his ultimate affirmation in Jesus Christ's death and resurrection" (Sperry 1978, 172-73). Because we have been affirmed, we are likewise able to affirm a counselee and to extend the offer of God's affirmation.

SUMMARY

In summary, the last three chapters have presented those characteristics of a counselor that allow the counselor to develop a healing relationship with the counselee. It has been pointed out that the counselee needs to be aware of a need and must desire to do something about the need for effective counseling to take place. The relationship between the counselor and counselee based on a model of mutual respect, grounded on trust and acceptance, has been presented. The approach to counseling developed is based on reason, reality, and responsibility. Finally, this chapter deals with our religious resources as counselors and our need to utilize them properly in effective counseling. The theoretical approach developed in these chapters is based on relationship, responsibility, and religion. The purpose of this approach is to provide guidance as we engage in the ministry of counseling.

DISCUSSION QUESTIONS

1. Can you think of any additional distinctives between Christian and secular counseling other than those suggested by Oates?
2. Suggest some resources of the Christian faith, other than those mentioned, that might be used in counseling.
3. Is it important for a Christian counselor to be filled with the Holy Spirit? Why?
4. Why does a Christian counselor need a good understanding of Scripture?
5. What is your reaction to Gary Collins's caution about the use of spiritual resources?

SUGGESTED READING

Graham, Billy. *The Holy Spirit*. Waco, Texas: Word Book Publishers, 1978. A balanced and easily read treatment of the person and work of the Holy Spirit.

Hadidian, Allen. *Successful Discipling*. Chicago: Moody, 1979. A good book on the art of one-on-one discipling. Discipling may be seen as a form of guidance counseling where the goal is spiritual growth.

McPhee, Arthur G. *Friendship Evangelism*. Grand Rapids: Zondervan, 1978. An interesting approach to sharing one's faith. Many of the principles discussed in this work are applicable to the counseling ministry.

Narramore, Clyde M. *The Psychology of Counseling*. Grand Rapids: Zondervan, 1960. A good appendix on the use of Scripture in counseling.

Ward, Waylon O. *The Bible in Counseling*. Chicago: Moody, 1977. A basic discussion of the role of Scripture in counseling. The major contribution of this work is the study guides on Scripture for counseling problems. The guides are made to be duplicated and given to counselees as homework.

CHAPTER SIX

Guidance Counseling

Ralph Cass, a high school senior, approaches Jim Taylor, his Sunday school teacher, after class and asks if they can talk. Ralph explains that he has been awarded an athletic scholarship to the state university. His parents would like him to attend the Bible college associated with their denomination and have offered to pay his tuition. However, they have said the decision is his and they will go along with whatever he decides. Ralph asks Jim Taylor for help in making the decision.

Sally Roberts has been an assistant manager for an employment office for several years. One evening she calls one of her friends from church and asks if she can come over and talk. When she arrives, Sally tells her friend that she has been offered a position as manager with a competing firm. Sally wants some advice on whether or not to accept the new offer.

Julie Swenson, a middle-aged mother, has seen her youngest child off to college. With fewer responsibilities around the home she would like to return to work. She has a degree in teaching but has not taught for 18 years. State laws have changed since she was certified, and she would need to pick up several courses to be certified again. Julie asks her husband what he thinks she should do.

What do Ralph, Sally, and Julie have in common? They are all seeking guidance counseling. Most lay counseling will fall into one of two areas: guidance counseling or crisis counseling.* This chapter examines guidance counseling and the next chapter, crisis counseling. Guidance counseling may be defined as the systematic process of aiding individuals to make choices and plans, as well as adjustments, in meeting the decisions involved in personal living. Guidance counseling may cover many areas such as educational, vocational, ethical, financial, and marital (Brammer 1973, 142).

It is important that we understand what guidance counseling is. Guidance counseling is not telling others what to do. Guidance counseling is not imposing our point of view on others or making decisions for others. Rather, guidance counseling is assisting others to make rational decisions in light of reality and the Word of God. It is helping others to develop *their* plan of action. Effective help for others should follow four principles of guidance counseling. Again, as with all areas of counseling, these principles build on the relationship between the counselor and counselee. The four principles are: (1) define the situation, (2) delineate the options, (3) develop the resources, and (4) delegate the responsibility.

DEFINE THE SITUATION

The second and third steps of applying Reality Therapy (see chapter 4) suggest examination and evaluation. The situation needs to be examined and defined before

---

*Crisis counseling has both a general and specific usage. Here it is used in a general way; it is used more specifically in chapter 7.

the options can be explored. There are two questions that can help define the situation.

WHAT IS THE PROBLEM?

If there were no problem or conflict the person would not be seeking guidance counseling. Let us take, for example, the case of Ralph Cass. If he wants to attend Bible college and his parents want him to, there should be no problem. On the other hand, if he wants to accept the athletic scholarship and his parents feel the same, there will be no problem. However, Ralph finds the athletic scholarship an attractive offer, but he also wants to please his parents. The problem needs to be defined clearly so that a realistic decision is possible.

WHAT IS THE GOAL OR PURPOSE?

Quite often a person becomes so involved in the immediacy of the decision process that sight is lost of goals. In counseling Ralph Cass, we would want to know what his purpose is for attending college. What are his goals related to a college education? Sometimes just clarifying one's goals makes the correct choice obvious. Julie Swenson wants to go back to work but finds she needs extra education to get back into teaching. Her dilemma revolves around whether or not it is worth it to pick up the extra courses. Knowing her goals may make the answer obvious. If her goal is to get back into teaching then she will have to take the courses. However, if her goal is to work outside the home and she has only thought of teaching because she already has a degree in that area then she needs to delineate all her options.

DELINEATE THE OPTIONS

Once a person's goals or purpose has been established, the next step is to delineate the options or ways of reaching the goals. If Julie Swenson's goal is to work outside the home in general rather than specifically return to teaching, she needs to find out what her options are. What is the market for school teachers? What other types of jobs are available? How accessible are the courses she would need to return to teaching?

People, when they are caught up in a situation, frequently only consider the apparent options. Counselors can help them discover other possibilities. As we look at the case of Ralph Cass, we might ask if there is a Christian college with athletic scholarships. Ralph Cass has only contrasted the state school or the Bible college. Julie Swenson has considered only teaching as a job outside the home. We need to guide people into considering all the options available. We should first ask counselees if they can think of any other options. When the counselee has either said there are no other options or listed some, then we may suggest any he or she is not aware of. It is important to let the counselees develop as many options as they can on their own. People are more likely to consider options they have come up with. When raising options with counselees, we should phrase them as questions such as, "Have you considered such and such," or "What would happen if you did this or that?" Once all the options have been delineated, the resources for evaluating the options can be developed.

DEVELOP THE RESOURCES

In order to evaluate the options under consideration, resources are usually required. Poor decisions are often based on a lack of information. Each of the options presented needs to be researched. Julie Swenson needs to know where and when the courses she requires for teacher certification are offered. She needs to know the cost of the courses and how long it will take her to complete them. She needs to know the employment possibilities in teaching. She needs to know if other jobs would be available to her without further education. She should know the pay, responsibilities, hours, and other pertinent information about them.

One of the most basic resources for evaluating options is a sheet of paper and a pen. Sally Roberts has received a job offer and is having a problem deciding whether or not she should take it. We suggest she take a sheet of paper and fold it in half. On one side she should list the advantages of staying in her present job. On the other side she should list the advantages of the new job. By listing the advantages of each job she will be able to compare them side by side. One is usually not able to keep all these items in mind at the same time, so writing them down allows one to consider them all.

Writing out ideas allows the person to literally see what he or she is thinking. Sometimes this can be a real discovery. After the counselee has completed the list, it would be appropriate for us to raise any additional advantages the counselee may have overlooked. When a decision involves only one option, that is whether or not to pursue a particular course of action, then the lists should involve the advantages and disadvantages of that course of action.

People are an important resource in decision making. It might be suggested to Ralph Cass that he talk to some students in the athletic program at the state university and to some students at the Bible college. Julie Swenson might consider talking with some teachers who have returned to teaching after an absence of several years. Sally Roberts might talk to other managers at the firm that has offered her the job.

There are many resources that a counselor and counselee can utilize in evaluating the options. The more research that is put into each option the better the evaluation process will be. It is important that counselors and counselees do not just sit around and share ignorance and biases with each other. They need to acquire the facts upon which a rational decision can be made. As we pointed out in chapter 2, God created humans as rational beings, and the intellectual faculties He has given us need to be used.

Two additional resources for Christian counselors and counselees are the Bible and prayer. For the Christian, these resources are not something added on to the evaluation process, but basic to it. The Bible has much to say about the decisions and choices Christians make. A girl graduated from a Christian college with a degree in teaching and wanted a job in her home town. When she applied there were no openings so she accepted a teaching position in another town. Shortly after signing her contract, a position became available in her home town. With little thought she broke her contract to take the job in her home town. The Bible teaches that when we make a promise we should keep it, even if it works to our disadvantage (Ps. 15:4). The decision of that girl violated a biblical principle of ethics. Christians need to evaluate their options in light of the ethical principles of Scripture.

Prayer also needs to be an important part of the decision-making process for Christians. A counselor and counselee should pray for God's wisdom and direction as they gather information and evaluate options. They should pray for understanding of the Scripture relevant to the decision. They should pray for the strength and courage to make morally right decisions. Christian counselors should also rely on their religious resources.

DELEGATE THE RESPONSIBILITIES

The final decision always should be the counselee's. We can guide, probe, raise issues, make suggestions, question options, but we must ultimately delegate the responsibility for the decision to the counselee. Counselees sometimes will try to get us to make the decision for them. Other times we will be greatly tempted to make the decision. However, the decision must be the counselee's. The counselee is the one who has to live with the decision.

There are several reasons why we should not make a decision for a counselee. One is that counselees are likely to blame us if the decision does not work out, rather than accepting the responsibility themselves. Another reason is that it tends to make counselees dependent. They need to learn to make their own decisions. In fact, the counseling process can also be educational as it teaches counselees how to go about making their own decisions. A third reason is that when counselees make their own decisions they have more motivation for following through. Still another reason is that if counselees do not make their own decisions their self-image may be affected. They may begin to question their ability to do so or view themselves as not worthwhile enough to do so. A final reason is that the Bible teaches that all will be held accountable for their own actions; therefore, the counselees need to make these decisions.

DISCERN THE WILL OF GOD

For the Christian counselee, the will of God must be a major consideration in any decision. As Christian counselors, we need to be able to guide a counselee in discerning the will of God. First of all, we need to realize that God has a plan for the lives of believers (Eph. 2:10). Next, the Bible tells us that God will reveal His will or plan for us (Ps. 32:8; Prov. 3:5-6). Then, God commands us to know and obey His will (Eph. 5:17; 6:6). While God has a will or plan for each believer, we need to recognize that in many cases it is general rather than specific. For example, we know it is God's will for us to take care of our bodies, which includes proper nutrition. However, within that general will, He leaves the specifics up to us. He expects us to use our common sense.

We would like to suggest there are at least four ways that God guides us or shows us His will. The first way is through His *Word*, the Bible, which reveals a significant part of God's will. The Bible instructs us in many areas of life including home, work, friends, worship, and service. The Scripture's directions for us, in most of these areas, are in the form of general principles rather than specifics. However, these principles can be applied to the specifics. In using Scripture to discern God's will it is important that we do not take verses out of context. We need to follow basic rules of biblical interpretation.

Another way God guides us is through *prayer*. As we pray about a matter God may make His will known to us. He may give us peace about the right decision and unrest over a wrong decision. The Holy Spirit may bring conviction on the matter to show us His will.

A third way God directs us is through *circumstances*. Circumstances include things such as being in the right place at the right time. Circumstances also involve "open doors" and "closed doors." We also include people's interests, abilities, and training under circumstances. Our aptitudes and abilities have been given to us by God for a purpose. Often Christians believe that God's will goes against their interests; however, that is not consistent with the God seen in the Bible. The Bible teaches that God loves us and wants us to have the desires of our hearts (Ps. 37:4-5).

Finally, God guides us through the *counsel* of other Christians. Believers make up the body of Christ and are to minister to each other. God usually works through human instruments. The counsel of other believers can often be used by God to direct us. The healing relationship can be used of God to provide guidance for His children.

A word of caution must be added about the last two ways God leads us, circumstances and counsel of others. Both of these need to be consistent with the teachings of Scripture. Circumstances and counsel that go contrary to the Word of God are not His will.

This chapter presents four basic principles of guidance counseling: define the problem, delineate the options, develop the resources for evaluation, and delegate the responsibility. It has also discussed how to discern God's will. The 3Rs—relationship, responsibility, and religion—all come into play in guidance counseling. Those of us who are involved in a ministry of counseling need to be ready to offer guidance to individuals as they make choices and plans for their lives.

DISCUSSION QUESTIONS

1. *Have you been approached by someone with problems that called for guidance counseling? What was the nature of these problems?*
2. *Why might just defining the situation, in some instances, make the correct choice obvious?*
3. *Is it better for the counselor or the counselee to research the various options in a decision? Why?*
4. *Are there ever any circumstances where a counselor should make a decision for a counselee? Give examples.*
5. *In what additional ways does God show us His will?*

SUGGESTED READING

Arnold, John D. and Tompkins, Bert. *How to Make the Right Decisions.* Milford, Mich.: Mott Media, 1982. A biblical and practical approach to decision making in one's own life as well as helping others make decisions. A case study approach makes it easy to follow and apply the principles.

Baxter, J. Sidlow. *Does God Still Guide?* Grand Rapids: Zondervan, 1971. A treatment by a well-known evangelical of God's leading in the lives of Christians. Well worth applying to your own life and counseling.

Bolles, Richard N. *What Color Is Your Parachute?* Berkeley, Calif.: Ten Speed Press, 1981. A very interesting approach to vocational decision making. The principles in this book are applicable to many areas of life.

Friesen, Gary. *Decision Making and the Will of God: A Biblical Alternative to the Traditional View.* Portland, Ore.: Multnomah, 1980. A different view of the Christian's responsibility to make good choices. Applying practical biblical principles is an essential aspect of decision making.

Mickelsen, A. Berkeley and Mickelsen, Alvera. *Better Bible Study: A Layman's Guide to Interpreting and Understanding God's Word.* Ventura, Calif.: Regal, 1977. Basic principles for interpreting the Bible. Since the Bible contains instructions on God's will for us we need to know how to understand it.

Smith, M. Blaine. *Knowing God's Will: Biblical Principles of Guidance.* Downers Grove, Ill.: InterVarsity, 1979. Handling decisions in life that are not directly covered in the Bible. Smith applies principles from Scripture to these situations.

CHAPTER SEVEN

Crisis Counseling

Mrs. Smith slammed on her brakes, but not in time to avoid running into the bike and child that had shot out from behind a parked car. Mrs. Smith felt nauseated and was trembling as she opened her car door. She staggered to the front of her car and felt a wave of dizziness as she saw the crumpled, bleeding body of a young girl. As help arrived, Mrs. Smith was talking incoherently and was not able to give the police much information. The child was rushed to a hospital where examination revealed a number of lacerations, but no permanent or disabling injuries. Mrs. Smith did not receive a citation because, as far as the police could determine, she was operating her car in a legal manner at the time of the accident.

Each of us is confronted at some time or another with events or situations that are disturbing to the point of threatening our sense of well-being and security. The magnitude of events sufficient to be disruptive varies from person to person. For some it might be the marriage of a son or daughter, for others the diagnosis of a serious illness or involvement in a serious accident, for still others it might be the discovery of free time in the early stages of retirement. Whatever the event or situation, and however routine or minor it may appear to someone else, to the person in crisis it is a real problem.

DEFINITION OF CRISIS

A crisis is any event or situation for which a person's normal coping mechanisms are inadequate. The event or situation may be dramatic or ordinary. It may involve many persons or only one individual. However, if it results in a problem for which one's normal problem-solving abilities are insufficient, it is a crisis for that person. Lawrence Brammer defines a crisis as, "A state of disorganization in which the helpee faces frustration ... or profound disruption of his ... methods of coping with stress" (Brammer 1973, 114).

In identifying a crisis, it is especially important that we utilize all of our listening skills. What may seem routine or ordinary to us may indeed be a crisis for the counselee. The counselee may present the situation in vague or specific terms. In either case the important thing is that this event or situation is causing the person a problem. It is our job, as counselors, to listen carefully and sincerely to determine the nature of the crisis for the individual.

In defining crises, authorities generally distinguish between two types of crises. In her book, *People in Crisis*, Lee Ann Hoff identifies these two types: developmental crises and situational crises (Hoff 1978).

DEVELOPMENTAL CRISES

Developmental crises are those crises that arise out of the process of maturing and making transitions through the various stages of life. They involve events such as starting school, puberty, dating, graduation, vocational changes, marriage, parenting, middle age, retirement, and facing one's own death. Speaking of developmental crises, C. W. Brister, a professor of pastoral counseling, says:

> Life thrusts these acts of being upon mankind, requires major decisions in each epoch, and issues in some form of character growth or failure. Each of these experiences is crucial in that it involves appropriate spiritual response, i.e., responsible behavior, at the right time in the course of one's pilgrimage. Such eras of change and growth may be regarded as creative crises when they prompt a person to place his life "in God's hands" (Ps. 31:15). Conversely, one who clutches life in his own hands is lost both to the human community and to the kingdom of God (Luke 9:24-25), (Brister 1964, 231).

We have the opportunity to help people work through the most common crises people face as they experience life changes. However, to do so we must be prepared. This involves being knowledgeable about the stages of human development and their normal characteristics and crises. At the end of the chapter, we will suggest some readings in this area. Some developmental crises involve decision making; for these situations please refer to the principles of guidance counseling in chapter 6.

SITUATIONAL CRISES

The second type of crisis is the situational crisis. Lee Ann Hoff describes a situational crisis as

> one that occurs as a result of some unanticipated traumatic event that is usually beyond one's control. Since it is unforeseen, generally there is nothing one can do to prepare for it. Some common situational crises are: loss of a parent through death or divorce, loss of a job or status, urban dislocation, fire, natural disaster, diagnosis of a chronic or fatal disease. The occurrence

*of one of these events may or may not result in a crisis
. . . much depends on the individual's personal and
social resources at the time (Hoff 1978, 11-12).*

Professor Howard Clinebell of the School of Theology
at Claremont calls these crises, "accidental crises"
(Clinebell 1979, 56). The case of Mrs. Smith is an example of a situational or accidental crisis. Her running
into the child on the bicycle was unanticipated and traumatic. There was nothing she could do to prepare for it.
We need to be ready to minister to persons who face
situational or accidental crises.

CHARACTERISTICS OF CRISES

The Chinese language gives us a vivid idea of two com-
plementary aspects of crises. The Chinese word for crisis
is made up of two pictographs. The first is the character
for "danger." The second is the character for "opportunity." The Chinese see crisis as composed of these two
diverse elements, the one threatening and the other providing the basis for growth and development.

Speaking of the opportunity aspect of crisis, Howard
Clinebell says,

*When a severe crisis strikes, life challenges us to turn
to people for support, to struggle and learn new coping
skills. If we do this, we develop stronger resources for
handling the next crisis. . . . One stands at a fork in the
path. One direction leads toward growth, the other
toward diminished effectiveness in handling life con-
structively. People can use crises growth fully only
if they can activate the energies of realistic hope in the
context of caring relationships (Clinebell 1979, 56-57).*

Every crisis that carries us beyond our ability to cope,
while threatening our deepest sense of well-being and
security, is also an opportunity to grow. Every crisis can
be viewed as a stepping stone in a person's discovery of

God's care and provision. The apostle Paul describes his own depression from crisis as an opportunity to test his hope in Him who is able even to raise the dead (2 Cor. 1: 8-11). Even so we are privileged to help people through developmental and situational crises to new plateaus of wholeness and faith in God. This is the essence of the healing relationship.

PHASES OF A CRISIS

Much research on crisis events over the past few decades indicates that such events are usually self-limiting in terms of time and are worked out through specific phases. A crisis normally lasts from one to six weeks after the event that caused it. During this period of time the person is often in a state of disequilibrium, but is striving to restore equilibrium. He or she may come through the crisis with unchanged functioning ability, or with a weakened or strengthened ability to cope. The counselee has this brief period, when his or her life is very malleable, to avoid regression and to actually achieve new and stronger functioning abilities.

Dr. Gerald Caplan of the Harvard School of Public Health describes four phases of a crisis (Caplan 1964, 40-41).

First, there is the original rise in tension from the problem stimulus, the experience of anxiety, perceived threat to self. This calls forth the habitual problem-solving responses which have been learned previously and which might be generalized to this particular problem stimulus.

Second, because of the novelty of the situation and the continuing intensity of the stimulus, there is a lack of success in reducing the anxiety with the usual coping mechanisms in the period of time expected. A feeling of helplessness and ineffectualness results.

Third, this is the "hitching up the belt" stage. The person dips deep into his reserve of strength and extends the range of his behavior in attempting to maintain his ego integrity. A redefinition of the problem may bring it into the range of prior experience. Trial and error behavior, both in thinking and in overt act, seeks to change or remove the problem stimulus. There may be a redefinition of one's role, thus a modification of identity. Active resignation may be integrated into the self image. The problem may be solved in this phase. If it is, the person usually becomes stronger, he moves farther along the continuum toward mental health, in that he has learned methods of dealing effectively with a new and threatening situation and has now brought this new learning into his repertoire of responses.

Fourth, if the problem continues with no need satisfaction, the tension produced by the anxiety may take the person beyond the threshold of rational responding, described by the term personality decompensation, where there are exaggerated distortions of one's identity or of the situation, rigid and compulsive and ineffective behavior, socially unacceptable behavior, extreme withdrawal, et cetera.

It is during Caplan's third phase of a crisis that counseling can be most effective. During this stage the individual will either grow or regress. If a person moves into Caplan's fourth stage he or she should immediately be referred to a competent professional (see chapter 13 on making referrals).

CRISIS INTERVENTION

The task of crisis intervention, in general and especially during the initial stages, is to provide a sense of supportive understanding ("I thank God that someone hears me and seems to understand what I am going through"), an opportunity to vent feelings ("I could even let myself cry without being ashamed"), and a sense of hope ("I began to realize that with God's help and your support I was going to make it"). Again, this is a function of the healing relationship.

The seven steps of Reality Therapy (see chapter 4) are particularly applicable to crisis counseling, as Brammer points out, because the crisis is the person's reaction to events and situations, not the events or situations themselves (Brammer 1973, 114). While counselees may not have any control over events and situations, they can control their reactions. Besides the seven steps of Reality Therapy, five principal tasks in crisis intervention may be suggested.

1. The counselee needs to gain insight on what has taken place and why it is so personally threatening. The counselor should aid the counselee in discovering these insights rather than by supplying them.

2. The counselor needs to let the counselee talk out his or her feelings and express emotions. The principles of effective listening discussed in chapter 3 are well applied here. It is important to let the counselee talk the feelings out rather than the counselor talking them out of the counselee.

3. The counselor needs to help the counselee "build a fence" around the event or situation by utilizing or developing an adequate support system. Religious resources are important here, especially the body of local believers.

4. The counselee needs to be helped to develop specific goals for dealing with the crisis. These goals should be consistent with biblical principles.

5. Toward the end of the crisis counseling it will be helpful to work through some "what if" exercises

with the counselee. This will allow the counselee to consolidate what has been learned from the present crisis and help the counselee cope with future crises.

Crises are a regular part of life and we need to be ready to reach out to help individuals as they encounter them. The following chapters consider some specific types of developmental and situational crises.

DISCUSSION QUESTIONS

1. Define a crisis.
2. What crises have you experienced in your life? Have you experienced a crisis that others thought was "not a big thing"? What was your reaction?
3. What growth coming out of crisis experiences have you witnessed in yourself or someone else?
4. Are you surprised by Paul's crisis in 1 Corinthians 1:8-11? What was the result for him? What does he suggest as a general outcome for other Christians (v. 10)?
5. How would you counsel with Mrs. Smith in the anecdote that opens this chapter?

SUGGESTED READING

1. Works on Crisis Counseling

Hoff, Lee Ann. People in Crisis. Reading, Mass.: Addison-Wesley, 1978. Good introduction to the study of crisis. A treatment useful for lay counselors.

Parad, Howard V. Crisis Intervention. New York: Family Service Association of America, 1965. Basic aspects of crisis intervention.

Switzer, David K. The Minister as Crisis Counselor. Nashville: Abingdon, 1965. A book written for pastors, with much material equally applicable to lay counselors.

2. Works on the Stages of Life
Childhood

Bee, Helen. *The Developing Child.* 3rd ed. New York: Harper & Row, 1981. A readable introduction to child development. This book covers physical, cognitive, and social development.

Bigner, J. J. *Parent-Child Relations.* New York: MacMillan, 1979. A work that deals with the parent-child relationship through various stages of child development.

Elder, C. A. *Values and Moral Development in Children.* Nashville: Broadman, 1976. A consideration of how children acquire values and develop moral thinking.

Kiley, Dan. *Nobody Said It Would Be Easy.* New York: Harper & Row, 1978. Written by a practicing child psychologist. The book deals with raising responsible children.

Satir, V. *Peoplemaking.* Palo Alto, Calif.: Science and Behavior Books, 1972. A classic and valuable book on childrearing. The last chapter of this book detracts from an otherwise useful work and should be ignored.

Adolescence

Conger, J. J. *Adolescence and Youth.* 2nd ed. New York: Harper & Row, 1977. A basic introduction to adolescent development.

Erickson, E. *Identity: Youth and Crisis.* New York: Norton, 1968. A classic treatment of adolescent development from a Neo-Freudian perspective.

Middle Age

Clinebell, H. J., Jr. *Growth Counseling for Mid-years Couples.* Philadelphia: Fortress, 1977. Valuable insights into this stage of life.

Howe, R. *The Creative Years.* Greenwich: Seabury, 1959. A unique approach to middle age. This book is delightful and insightful reading.

Sheehy, G. *Passages.* New York: Dutton, 1976. A National bestseller. This is a popularized version of a scientific study on mid-life crises.

Retirement and Aging

Bengston, V. *The Social Psychology of Aging.* Indianapolis: Bobbs-Merrill, 1973. Coverage of sociological as well as psychological aspects of aging.

Kennedy, C. E. *Human Development: The Adult Years and Aging.* New York: MacMillan, 1978. A basic introduction to this stage of life.

CHAPTER EIGHT

Grief, Death, and Dying

There is a time for everything,
and a season for every activity under heaven:
a time to be born and a time to die. . . .
a time to weep and . . .
a time to mourn. . . . (Eccles. 3:1-4)

Grief is more common in the lives of individuals than most of us realize. As R. Scott Sullender, a clinical psychologist, reminds us,

Surely everyone will eventually know the grief that comes in response to the death of someone dearly loved. Many will grieve the loss of a marital relationship in separation and/or divorce. But amid these larger griefs, there are also the smaller common griefs of everyday living. Inevitably most people will change jobs or homes and know the grief that comes in response to the loss of the familiar. Every time people visit an airport, train station or bus depot, they give expression to grief as friends and family arrive and depart. Like the air, grief is so common in human experience that we seldom notice it except in tragic circumstances (Sullender 1980, 33:243).

[103]

A DEFINITION OF GRIEF

While grief is a common emotion which most of us have experienced, it is a difficult concept to define. Grief is a process that varies from person to person and situation to situation. Sullender points out three major theoretical approaches to understanding the grief process. Grief may be seen as a reaction to loss, as a separation anxiety, and as a function of attachment (Sullender 1980, 33:243). Each approach has its strengths and weaknesses. We will briefly examine each approach so that we may use the strengths of each in order to further our understanding of grief.

GRIEF AS A REACTION TO LOSS

The most common approach to understanding grief is to view it as an emotional reaction to the loss of a person or thing. The loss of a person may result from death, a move, a divorce, or other causes. The loss of things may include physical objects such as a family heirloom, a car wrecked in an accident, or any other physical object of value. "Things" may also include the nonmaterial—such as holding a job, making a sports team, maintaining one's reputation, or enjoying any other valued or desired event or position. Sullender notes that among the events that are rated highest on the Holmes-Rahe Social Readjustment Rating Scale (a test for measuring the stressfulness of various life events, see Table 9-1 in chapter 9), the majority involve loss—death, divorce, marital separation, jail term, etc. (Sullender 1980, 33:244). The strength of this approach to understanding grief is that it reminds us which life events may cause grief.

GRIEF AS SEPARATION ANXIETY

A second major approach to understanding grief is to view it as a separation anxiety. Separation anxiety is basically a fear (often vague and undefinable) of separation from a significant other or others. Separation anxiety begins in infancy. We have all observed a young child scream when his or her mother leaves the room. That fear of being cut off from significant others continues throughout life (witness the homesickness of college students). As chapter 2 points out, God has created humans as social beings with a need to relate to others.

One strength of this approach is to focus on the person experiencing the grief. We must recognize that the person feels threatened by the events causing the grief and may react in fear. Another strength of this approach is that it reminds us of the importance of providing support for the individual. This is an area where the church, as a community of empathetic brothers and sisters, can play a significant role.

GRIEF AS A FUNCTION OF ATTACHMENT

The third major approach for understanding grief is to view it as a function of attachment. In this view grief is not caused by the loss but by the value placed on the person or thing lost. When humans lose a person or thing to which they are attached they still have the feelings and emotions of attachment with no object. Grief then is the gradual and painful process of withdrawal of the emotional investment made in the lost person or thing. A person then needs to work through the process of withdrawing his or her emotional investment in the lost person or thing before he or she is able to reinvest in another person or thing.* One strength of this approach is that it

_____

*Sometimes a person may attempt to reinvest the emotional attach-

allows us to view grief as a process. Another strength is its emphasis on value and emotional investment made; the greater the value and/or emotional investment, the greater the grief.

A complete understanding of grief needs to take into account all three of these theoretical approaches. We need to be aware of the causes of grief—what are the precipitating events? We also need to focus on the person experiencing the grief rather than on the event. It is important to provide empathetic support. We need to also view grief as a process of emotional disattachment. With these three perspectives in mind we can go on to discuss the stages of grief, the needs of the grieving, and some guidelines for counseling the grieving.

THE STAGES OF GRIEF

Gary Collins suggests that there are three stages of grief: shock, intense grief, and readjustment (Collins 1972, 145-46).

SHOCK

When confronted with a traumatic loss, the first reaction of many persons is shock, or numbness. There is no reaction at all. Often defense mechanisms will come into play immediately to protect the person. One of the most common is denial. The person denies the loss has taken place (e.g., "There has been a mistake, it is another Mr. Smith who was killed"). A more subtle form of denial

---

ment of a lost person or thing to a new one. An example is a "rebound marriage" where a person who has lost a mate through death or divorce immediately remarries. This strategy for dealing with grief is usually unhealthy and harmful. It usually leads to greater problems.

may involve preoccupation with the details of the situation in order to avoid facing reality. As the person begins to accept reality, there may be physical symptoms such as dizziness or fainting, headache, nausea, or shortness of breath. The shock stage usually is brief, lasting a few hours to a few days.

INTENSE GRIEF

The stage of intense grief is often marked by uncontrolled emotional responses. These may range from continuous weeping to intense rage. Depression is also common during this stage (see chapter 9 for a fuller discussion of depression as a result of loss). Some Christians may feel anger or resentment toward God for allowing the loss. There is often a good deal of questioning, "Why did God allow this?" or "Why did this happen to me?"

Another common reaction during this stage is guilt. Some persons may feel responsible for the loss, whether or not they really are. There may also be guilt over past treatment of a lost one. Again, we must distinguish between real and false guilt (see chapter 2 for a discussion of the distinction). For real guilt there is confession, forgiveness, and reconciliation through Christ.

READJUSTMENT

The grieving person moves gradually from the intense grief stage into a period of readjustment. The intense grief stage normally lasts from a few days to several weeks. It is generally agreed that it takes at least a year to work through the grief of a major loss. Yet, in most cases, support is withdrawn from grieving persons after the intense grief stage. When the crying has stopped, many people assume the person is done grieving and can make it on his or her own. However, authorities are coming to see the period of readjustment, which can last a year or more, as the most critical stage of grief. During the first two stages we can do little more than provide comfort and support. However, it is during the readjustment stage that there is the greatest potential for growth. It is at this stage that the healing relationship can be most beneficial. We need to recognize that grief is a process that moves through various stages, and it is important to provide the appropriate ministries for each stage.

NEEDS OF THE GRIEVING

Persons experiencing grief have some specific needs. W. F. Rogers, a hospital chaplain, has suggested five needs of those who grieve (Rogers 1963, 14:19-26).

SUPPORT

The first need of a grieving person is support from others. The person who is experiencing grief has lost some of his or her regular support. The need is for others to provide that support. The support may be material such as fixing meals and caring for children. It may involve being there, just listening. While the needs may vary, the support is necessary. This need continues through the various stages and in varying degrees and may last as long as twenty-four months.

ACCEPTANCE OF REALITY

Acceptance of reality needs to take place on two levels, the intellectual and the emotional. A discussion of the defense mechanisms people use to avoid reality and how to help them is given in chapter 4. Emotional acceptance usually takes longer than intellectual acceptance; it is part of the withdrawal of the emotional investment discussed earlier.

EXPRESSION OF SORROW

The grieving person needs to express sorrow. Expressing sorrow is not a sign of weakness nor a sign of lack of spirituality or faith. When Jesus met Mary and Martha following the death of Lazarus, He wept (John 11:35). We need to avoid the temptation to tell the person to "be brave," "cheer up," or "have faith." Rather, we need to follow Paul's admonition to "weep with those who weep" (Rom. 12:15, AV). The need to express sorrow is legitimate and important, and we need to encourage and support it. If we do not allow a healthy expression of sorrow, it will come out in unhealthy ways.

EXPRESSION OF HOSTILITY AND GUILT

Anger and hostility are often reactions to frustration. There is little that is more frustrating than to experience a loss over which one has no control. Guilt is also a common reaction to grief. Whether the anger and/or guilt is justified or not, it needs to be expressed. It is only when it is brought out into the open that it can be dealt with. If we encourage a person to suppress his anger and/or guilt, it does not go away; it will come out in physical or psychological symptoms. We need to accept the person and his or her anger and/or guilt (remember acceptance does not mean approval or condoning; see chapter 3). It is only through expression and acceptance that the hostility and/or guilt can be dealt with in a healthy and constructive way.

NEW RELATIONSHIPS

Grief has been discussed as a function of attachment. As the person becomes emotionally detached from the lost person or thing, there is a need to help with the detachment process and to help in building new relationships. These new relationships need not be of the same type. For example, a widow might build new relationships with other widows rather than with a man.

COUNSELING THE GRIEVING

Because grief is not an event or situation, but the individual's reaction to the event or situation, we need guidelines for counseling the grieving. The seven steps of Reality Therapy (see chapter 4) may be applied to help the grieving evaluate their reaction to the situation and to make plans for coping with the situation. In addition to these steps there are four other guidelines for counseling the grieving, based on the earlier discussion of the essence of grief, its stages, and the needs of those experiencing grief.

BEING THERE

Our presence is very important in grief counseling—it requires a time commitment. Not only do we need to be there during the shock and intense grief stages, but we need to be there through the readjustment stage. Our sessions may be longer and more frequent during the first two stages, but we need to continue the counseling process through the readjustment stage. It is in this stage that we will have our greatest opportunities to provide constructive help for personal and spiritual growth.

LISTENING

While listening is important in all types of counseling, it is critical in grief counseling. Effective listening skills are discussed in chapter 3. During the second stage of intense grief, listening may be the most beneficial service we can provide. The better we listen, the better we will be able to help when the person is ready to look to the future.

PROVIDE SUPPORT

We need to be ready to provide support needed by the grieving. As Christian counselors we can mobilize the resources of the church to help provide the support. The church should be ready to help with meals, child care, transportation, or whatever else is needed. The members of the church should be able to provide emotional and spiritual support as well as material or physical needs.

USE SPIRITUAL RESOURCES

We should be using our spiritual resources in all of our counseling. However, in grief counseling, we need to be aware of how these resources may best be applied. Prayer can often be a source of strength and comfort. Scripture can offer both comfort and hope. However, we must be careful to use prayer and Scripture with sensitivity. The person whc is experiencing grief needs help, and as Christians we are in a unique position to minister to that individual.

DEATH AND DYING

One of the most traumatic causes of grief is death, both that of a loved one and facing our own. In recent years much research has been done on death and dying. One of the leading authorities in this field has been Elisabeth Kubler-Ross, a psychiatrist and family therapist. Her research has led her to conclude that there are five stages that most dying persons and their close family members go through (Kubler-Ross 1969, c. 3-7). Each of these five stages is considered here. However, not all dying persons or close family members go through each stage. Also, not all persons experience the stages in the same order. Nevertheless, many persons do go through all five stages in the given order.

DENIAL AND ISOLATION STAGE

The first reaction to the news of a terminal diagnosis, either for oneself or one's loved one, is often denial. Frequently we will hear statements such as, "The lab must have gotten the blood samples mixed up," or "They probably misread the X-ray," or "The doctor is an alarmist." Sometimes people will go from physician to physician seeking another diagnosis. Another more subtle form of denial involves going about business as usual while ignoring the facts or the reality of the diagnosis.

A person usually experiences shock when he hears of one's own or a loved one's impending death. Denial is a mechanism for handling shock. Norman Wright says, "Denial has been called the human shock absorber to tragedy" (Wright 1977, 134). Denial allows one to gradually adjust to trauma. Joyce Landorf, in her sensitive book, *Mourning Song*, shares the lesson she learned about denial in facing her mother's death:

I now know that denial is needed in our emotions to act as a buffer or safety zone after we see the reality of someone else's (or our own) death. It gives a temporary measure of healing. It can be used in our lives as a God-given diversion.

Somewhere along the line we as Christians have been given the general feeling that if you are a Christian denial is not a problem or, in some cases, shouldn't even exist. What happens when a Christian does experience denial? And what if, in his denial, his actions do not appear to be too Christian?

We need denial to help us through the most shocking moments of our painful knowledge.

We need denial—but we must not linger in it. We must recognize it as one of God's unique tools and use it. . . . We do not need to feel guilty or judge our level of Christianity. . . . However, after . . . the initial danger has passed, we need not be dependent on it (Landorf 1974, 47-53).

We need to recognize that denial is often a normal and healthy reaction to shock. It allows one to adjust gradually to the news of death. However, as Joyce Landorf has said, one needs to move from denial to reality. When a person persists in a state of denial and uses it as an escape from reality rather than a means for adjusting to reality then denial has ceased to be an aid and has become a problem. A person who persists in a state of denial usually needs professional help (see chapter 13 on making referrals).

One of the forms denial takes among the close family and friends of the dying person is isolation. The more one avoids, or isolates oneself from the dying person, the less one has to face the reality of that person's impending death. Unfortunately, this also isolates the dying person. Wright points out,

One of the problems that can occur is the Abandonment Syndrome. Dying people express the fear that their condition will make them so unacceptable to others around them that they will be abandoned, and in many cases studies have confirmed their fears.

Sometimes . . . terminally ill patients are actually

abandoned. . . . Often this is a reaction to the fears the
person has of one's own death. Because of the implica-
tions of the loved one's death, we have to try to sepa-
rate ourselves from him in some way (Wright 1977,
136).

Norman Cousins, a layman facing his own possible
death, wrote,

Death is not the ultimate tragedy of life. The ulti-
mate tragedy is depersonalization—dying in an alien
and sterile area, separated from the spiritual nourish-
ment that comes from being able to reach out to a lov-
ing hand, separated from a desire to experience the
things that make life worth living, separated from
hope (Cousins 1979, 133).

In counseling with the family of dying patients we
need to help them work through their denial as well as
the next three stages and arrive at acceptance. At that
point they will be able to provide support for the dying
loved one. We need to help the family avoid isolating the
dying patient.

ANGER STAGE

When the reality of one's own or a loved one's impending death breaks through the defense of denial and is
fully comprehended, the next reaction is frequently
anger. Death is frustrating, maybe the ultimate frustration, and anger is a normal reaction to frustration. The
target of the anger may be oneself, loved ones, the doctors and nurses, some unspecified target, or even God
himself. Job in his anguish said,

Therefore, I will not restrain my mouth;
I will speak in the anguish of my spirit,
I will complain in the bitterness of my soul.

(Job 7:11, NASB)

We often view these angry reactions as un-Christian,

especially if they are directed at God. Frequently we are disturbed by outbursts of anger toward God, not for His sake, but for our own. We find them threatening to us. We may harbor some suppressed resentment toward God and the other person's verbalization of his or her resentment taps into ours. This is why self-awareness and self-acceptance are so important for counselors. It is only when we are self-aware and self-accepting that we can accept the other person even when he or she is angry at God. It is only as we accept the other person in his or her anger, no matter who or what is the object of the anger, that we will be able to provide help.

BARGAINING STAGE

This stage usually follows the anger stage. People realize that anger, particularly toward God, is not going to do them any good. So they will try to bargain with God. "If you will only let me live a little longer, I'll serve you anywhere," or "If you let my loved one live, I will do such and such for you."

A classic example of bargaining is found in the Old Testament:

> In those days Hezekiah became ill and was at the point of death. The prophet Isaiah ... went to him and said, "This is what the Lord says: Put your house in order, because you will die; you will not recover."
>
> Hezekiah turned his face to the wall and prayed to the Lord, "Remember, O Lord, how I have walked before you faithfully and with wholehearted devotion and have done what is good in your eyes." And Hezekiah wept bitterly (2 Kings 20:1-3).

Turning to the New Testament we see several people who came to Jesus on behalf of ill or dying persons (e.g., the centurion, Matt. 8:5-13; Peter's mother-in-law, Matt. 8:14-15; Jairus's daughter, Mark 5:21-43; Lazarus, John

11). In each of these cases Jesus' response was positive.

What should be our reaction to persons who are bargaining with God for their own lives or those of loved ones? We need to recognize that God does answer prayer and is able to heal. We also need to recognize that everyone eventually dies. As Chris Lyons, pastor of the Wheaton Bible Church, Wheaton, Illinois, once stated it:

God heals you of every sickness but your last. For the Bible says, "It is appointed unto man to die." In other words, should Jesus Christ tarry, every one of us here tonight at some time is going to die. Some bodily organ will cease functioning—it will break down and we will die. Think of the healing results during the ministry of Jesus. There were lepers cleansed of their diseases, but they are not living today. Something else happened to them and they died. The woman with the issue of blood was healed of her disease but something else happened to her and eventually she died. They are not around today. God heals us of every disease, but "it is appointed unto man once to die" (Lyons 1973).

Well-meaning Christians often suggest that healing and recovery has not taken place because the person lacks faith or is practicing a sin he or she will not deal with. While sinful practices may result in physical illness, most illness is not the result of either sin or lack of faith. In 2 Corinthians 12:7-10, the apostle Paul tells of his physical ailment and how he prayed three times for healing. Paul did not lack faith (he had healed others and even raised the dead), and his illness was not the result of his sin. Rather, as Christians we must look to Paul's words in 1 Corinthians 15:50-57:

I declare to you, brothers, that flesh and blood cannot inherit the kingdom of God, nor does the perishable inherit the imperishable. . . . For the perishable must clothe itself with the imperishable, and the mortal with immortality. When the perishable has been

clothed with the imperishable, and the mortal with immortality, then the saying that is written will come true: "Death has been swallowed up in victory."
"Where, O death, is your victory?
    Where, O death, is your sting?"
The sting of death is sin, and the power of sin is the law. But thanks be to God! He gives us the victory through our Lord Jesus Christ.

DEPRESSION STAGE

By this stage people have exhausted most of their energy and resources. Reality has pushed through the defenses of denial, anger has depleted emotional resources, and bargaining has failed. At this point, depression sets in. A fuller discussion of depression is given in chapter 9.

How can we best minister to a person in this stage? Norman Wright suggests,

This is a time when the person needs to express sorrow and pour it out. We can minister best at this point by sitting silently with the person or holding his hand and letting him know that it is all right to express his feelings. Don't argue or debate with him, for the consequences can only be negative (Wright 1977, 135).

ACCEPTANCE STAGE

Chapter 9 points out that depression is usually self-limiting. As the people come out of the depression stage they often move into the acceptance stage. This is the point where the individual accepts his or her own or loved one's death. The person is at peace with himself and God.

Joyce Landorf describes her mother's acceptance of death,

During the last week of my mother's life, we could distinctly feel her God-given confidence in dying. Even though she did not always understand the ways and workings of God, she spent the last week alive and in great beauty. The dignity of her inner confidence was apparent to all who saw her (Landorf 1974, 113).

The person who is dying and the person's family may not go through the stages at the same time or rate. For example, the dying person may be questioning God in the anger stage. The family may be in the bargaining stage as they attempt to strike a bargain with God for the life of their loved one. The conflict that the dying person and the family will face is obvious; while one is challenging God, the others are petitioning God. We need to recognize that the various parties involved in a death may well go through the stages of dying at different rates and times. It should be pointed out that some individuals may become locked into one stage and not progress to the next.

JESUS AND DYING

Like everyone of us, Jesus had to face His death. It will be instructive for us to see how Jesus faced His death. As His death approached, Jesus did not want to be isolated; He wanted to be with His friends. Luke records Jesus saying, *I have eagerly desired to eat this Passover with you before I suffer* (Luke 22:15). Mark records that Jesus did not want to be alone as He grieved His death, *He took Peter, James and John along with him, and he began to be deeply distressed and troubled. "My soul is overwhelmed with sorrow to the point of death," he said to them* (Mark 14:33-34).

Mark then records that Jesus bargained with God. *Going a little farther, he fell to the ground and prayed that if possible the hour might pass from him. "Abba, Father," he said, "everything is possible for you. Take this cup* from me. Yet not what I will, but what you will" (Mark 14:35-36).

On the cross Jesus experienced depression as He called out, My God, my God, why have you forsaken me? (Mark 15:34). However, He quickly moved into acceptance of His death as witnessed by His words, Father, into your hands I commit my spirit (Luke 23:46).

We need to remember that while Jesus was the Son of God and divine, He was also fully human. As a human, Jesus faced death and as a human, He feared death. Also, as a human, He had to deal with His impending death. We should not be shocked or surprised that Jesus experienced the same emotions, as His death approached, that we experience. Rather, we should be encouraged and comforted. He understands what we are experiencing. The way Jesus faced His death can be a source of encouragement and comfort to those who are going through this experience.

DISCUSSION QUESTIONS

1. What are some grief experiences you have had? Which of the theoretical approaches best explains them?
2. Is it wrong for a grieving person to experience anger? Why?
3. Have you experienced the death of a loved one? If so, did you or the loved one go through Kubler-Ross's stages?
4. Is bargaining wrong for a Christian? Why?
5. What do you find most comforting in the fact that Jesus experienced the stages of dying?

SUGGESTED READING

Davidson, Glen W. *Living with Dying.* Minneapolis: Augsburg, 1975. A readable and helpful book for ministering to the dying.

Kubler-Ross, Elisabeth. *On Death and Dying.* New York: MacMillan, 1969; *Questions and Answers on Death and Dying.* New York: MacMillan, 1974; *Death: The Final Stage of Growth.* Englewood Cliffs, N.J.: Prentice-Hall, 1975. Three works presenting Kubler-Ross's stages of death and dying as well as her insights gained from working with the dying.

Landorf, Joyce. *Mourning Song.* Old Tappan, N.J.: Revell, 1974. A well-written account of the death of the author's mother. She traces her mother's passage through Kubler-Ross's stages. As Christians both the author and her mother demonstrated valuable insights to faith.

Yancey, Philip. *Where Is God When It Hurts?* Grand Rapids: Zondervan, 1977. A Christian perspective on the problem of pain and suffering.

Depression

Pauline "Polly" Larson died by her own hand on September 19, 1977. A Ph.D. candidate, a teaching assistant and supervisor of assistants at her university, she is described by her pastor as "a young woman of great intellect and gentleness of spirit, a scholar, a teacher and poet." She was a member of the North Park Covenant Church of Chicago and an associate member of the University Baptist Church of Champaign, Illinois. Polly was a victim of depression (Nelson 1979, 4).

DEFINITION OF DEPRESSION

We use the word *depression* in a variety of ways. It can be used to refer to anything from being a little "down," to severe emotional illness. The National Association for Mental Health defines depression as "an emotional state of dejection and sadness, ranging from mild discouragement and downheartedness to feelings of utter hopelessness and despair" (Brussel and Irwin 1973, 20).

Depression is a symptom of other problems. Norman Wright says that, "Depression is a signal that something in . . . life is not right" (Wright 1977, 70). He points out that depression is a response to what a person is doing with his or her life. Depression is a reaction. It is a message that something is wrong.

EXTENT OF DEPRESSION IN AMERICA

Who is it that suffers from depression? Just about everyone. It is the most common psychological disorder (Kline 1974, 9). One out of every eight Americans can expect to be treated for depression at some point in his or her lifetime (Wright 1977, 64). The National Institute for Mental Health states that eight million Americans are treated for depression each year (Brussel and Irwin 1973, 37). Of these, 300,000* need to be hospitalized (Wright 1977, 64). Depression is experienced by persons of every age and social class. While more than twice as many women as men are treated for depression, that does not mean that they are necessarily more susceptible to depression. Women may only be more likely to seek treatment for it. Twice as many men as women commit suicide, and depression is the leading cause of suicide (Minirth and Meier 1978, 20).

Depression is a widespread phenomenon. Many therapists find that persons with depression dominate their caseloads. As we get actively involved in lay counseling, we will find ourselves, sooner or later, dealing with depressed persons.

SYMPTOMS OF DEPRESSION

Depression can manifest itself in both physical and psychological symptoms. Counselors should have a

---

*These figures are probably low since family doctors sometimes admit depressed patients with another diagnosis.

familiarity with the more common symptoms in order to better understand their counselees. Physical and psychological symptoms are discussed separately, but it is important to remember they often appear together. These symptoms may appear individually or in any number of combinations.

PHYSICAL SYMPTOMS

Psychologists and medical doctors often refer to physical problems as psychosomatic. This term is derived from *psyche* referring to the mind and *soma* referring to the body.* It means physical manifestations with a psychological cause. When a person has the flu, there is a physical cause, namely a virus. When a person has an infection, there is a physical cause, namely a germ. When a person has a broken arm, there is a physical cause, namely an accident. However, a person may have an ulcer when there is no physical cause, no virus, no germ, no accident. The body has reacted to the mind. Depression may bring about many different physical changes.
Eating habits • When people are depressed their eating habits often change. They may have a loss of appetite. They may pick at their food and show no real interest in eating. On the other hand they may begin to gorge themselves as they turn to food for solace. Of the two changes, loss of appetite is the more common. While changes in eating habits may have many causes, they are a possible symptom of depression.
Sleeping habits • Depressed persons may also experi-

---

*Because some lay persons have misunderstood the term *psychosomatic* (thinking that it refers to symptoms that are not "real"), some professionals are using the term *psychogenic*. This term, with the ending derived from the word *genesis*, means beginning or originating in the mind.

ence changes in their sleeping habits. While some depressed persons may have trouble getting to sleep, it is more common for them to wake up during the night or very early in the morning and then not be able to get back to sleep. Other depressed persons may spend as much time as possible sleeping. This can be a form of escapism, in which they use sleep to escape from their problems. Escapism will be discussed under psychological symptoms.

Energy level • Persons who are depressed often act lethargic. They seem to have no energy. They may constantly complain of being tired. Quite often eating habits, sleeping habits, and level of energy will interact. Obviously eating and sleeping habits are going to affect levels of energy.

Sexual interest • Depression often affects sexual interest. Depressed persons may show an involuntary decline in their sexual interest. Depressed males may experience impotence. Depression can also affect the menstrual cycle. In cases of mild depression some men may become more sexually aggressive as a way of reaffirming their self-concept; however, depression usually leads to a lessening of sexual interest and activity.

Appearance • Depression can affect the way people care for themselves. Those who are usually neat and clean may begin to appear unkempt and sloppy if they are depressed. Depressed persons may lose interest or concern for their appearance.*

Physical Ailments • A number of physical ailments are common in depressed persons. Constipation as well as other gastric disturbances such as heartburn may be

---

*The main thing to look for in regard to sleep, eating habits, sexual interest, and appearance is *change* from previous patterns of behavior.

associated with depression. Other physical symptoms include chest pain, shortness of breath, and dizziness. While the above symptoms may all have physical causes or may be symptoms of a physical illness, they are also associated with depression. When they are symptoms of depression, they are usually associated with one or more of the psychological symptoms discussed below.

PSYCHOLOGICAL SYMPTOMS

Even as depression may manifest itself in various physical symptoms, it may also manifest itself in many psychological (behavioral and emotional) symptoms.
Feelings of sadness, hopelessness, despair, and apathy • Depressed persons have a pervading sense of gloom. They tend to be unhappy and pessimistic. Probably the most common feeling is one of helplessness. In fact, 75 percent of depressives who seek counseling feel they will never recover (Minirth and Meier 1978, 25). As one writer describes it, "Depression is a move toward deadness" (Wright 1977, 65).
Anxiety • One of the most distressing symptoms is that of feeling anxious. The depressed may complain that they feel "jittery" or that their minds are "racing." They often feel that some unknown tragedy is about to take place.
Loss of self-esteem • Depression can lead to a loss of self-confidence. When people are depressed they may begin to question their personal worth. Depressed people tend to view themselves as falling short of their own and others' expectations. People who are depressed may also feel that others see them as being of little worth. Depression often leads to a distortion of one's self-concept in a negative direction.
Loss of perspective • A very common symptom of depression is loss of perspective. It is very difficult for

depressed people to keep things in perspective. Minor incidents are treated as major catastrophes. The depressed often misinterpret what others say or do. They tend to interpret events in a negative way. They distort reality by not keeping reality in a proper perspective.

Loss of ambition and/or efficiency • People who are depressed, especially if they are usually "go-getters," often report that they have no drive. They lose interest in work, hobbies, or other interests that they normally find challenging. They often find themselves going in circles. They seem to have difficulty concentrating for any length of time on any one project.

Emotional overreaction • Depressed persons often overreact emotionally. They may cry "at the drop of a hat." They may lash out in anger at the slightest offense. They may laugh or smile at inappropriate times or they may laugh excessively over a minor point of humor. These emotional overreactions may be related to their loss of perspective. As perspective on situations is lost, the response to those situations will tend to be an overreaction. The overreaction may also be a cover-up for other feelings. For example, those who laugh excessively over a joke may be covering up a feeling of sadness.

Withdrawal • There is a tendency for depressed persons to want to withdraw from others. They often want to be left alone. They do not want to get out and mix with other people, even close friends and family. Depressed persons may attempt to isolate themselves from others by remaining in their rooms, not answering the phone, canceling appointments, and in other ways withdrawing physically. Depressed persons may also practice psychological withdrawal. That is, they may be physically present but mentally absent. They will ignore and not respond to those present, or their responses might be polite and superficial, designed to keep others at a distance.

Escapism • Depressed persons may attempt to escape from their problems. Escape may take many forms. It may begin in withdrawal. It may involve leaving home or running away. It may involve the ultimate form of escape, escape from life itself, suicide, a topic discussed at length in the next chapter.

Guilt • Guilt is frequently associated with depression. The guilt may be real or false. When the depressed lose perspective, they may feel guilt for things over which there is no need to feel guilt. Depressed persons often blame themselves for things for which they are not responsible, such as the death of a loved one. Whether real or imagined, guilt can be debilitating to a depressed person. It should be noted that depression is not a sin, although it may result from sin.

Dependence • Because depressed persons often feel helpless, they also often become dependent. Depressed persons can have a hard time making decisions, and they lean on others to make decisions for them.

Many of these symptoms of depression are also causes of depression. Once people begin to become depressed they will often behave in ways that reinforce the depression. This reaction to depression often deepens the depression. Depression seems to feed on itself and the cycle needs to be broken. However, before we can talk about breaking the cycle of depression, we need to look at the causes and consequences of depression. At this point we need to remember that depression is more than discouragement. We all get discouraged from time to time. Depression is a syndrome identified by a cluster of the previously discussed symptoms.

CAUSES OF DEPRESSION

As with the symptoms of depression, the causes of depression can be categorized as either physical or psychological. *Physical* means biological, and *psychological* means behavioral and emotional.

PHYSICAL CAUSES

In some cases depression may have a physical cause. It is important for a counselor to be aware of physical causes of depression. All the talk in the world will not help those who are depressed from physical causes. The most common physical causes of depression include diet, fatigue, drugs and alcohol, illness, and postpartum depression.

Diet • While the expression, "you are what you eat," is not the complete truth, it is true that what and how people eat does affect them. Those with irregular eating patterns and a poor diet are susceptible to wide mood swings.* People whose diet is low on protein or whose diet consists of junk food high in refined sugar may experience bouts of depression. Researchers are discovering that diet has a significant effect on emotional state.

Fatigue • People who do not get sufficient sleep over an extended period of time may become depressed. Those who continually take on physical demands beyond their capabilities may become depressed as a result of exhaustion. Some experts feel that fatigue is one of the most common causes of depression (Minirth and Meier 1978, 114). Many college students suffer depression because they try to "burn the candle from both ends." The average adult needs seven to eight hours of sleep a night. Without

---

*College students are particularly susceptible to this problem.

this rest, an individual is susceptible to depression.

Drugs and alcohol • Medication prescribed for physical problems can affect an individual's mood. All drugs have some effect on the body. If brain or nervous system toxicity results from the use of a drug, depression can develop. Some sedatives can cause depression when used for an extended period of time. Illegal or street drugs can also cause depression. For example, persons who use amphetamines ("speed," "pep pills," "uppers") regularly, often experience depression when the effects of the amphetamine wear off. Excessive use of caffeine (over 10 cups of coffee in 24 hours) can have an effect similar to amphetamines in some persons.

Alcoholism can also lead to depression. Continuous heavy drinking can produce chronic depression. When counseling with depressed people, counselors should always ascertain if they are taking any drugs, prescription or illegal, and if they are using alcohol and to what extent. Counselors need to be aware that depression may result from chemical reactions. Chemical dependency is discussed in chapter 13.

Physical illness • Depression may result from a physical illness and its effect on the body. Dr. Frank B. Minirth and Dr. Paul D. Meier point out "that depression often accompanies viral illness." They continue, "Viral illnesses can cause a temporary depressionlike syndrome" (Minirth and Meier 1978, 114). Depression is also common with hepatitis. Illnesses or injuries that involve a good deal of pain or discomfort can also lead to depression. The counselor needs to recognize that some depression may be a side effect of a physical illness.

Other medical conditions that can result in depression include hypoglycemia and a variety of glandular disorders. Hypoglycemia, or low blood sugar, is a pathological lowering of the level of sugar in the blood. (According to current medical opinion, this cause is quite rare.)

The most common cause of this problem is an elevation of insulin. Another possible cause is disturbed metabolism.

Glandular disorders that may result in depressive symptoms include hypo- or hyper-thyroidism, hormonal irregularities, imbalance in the secretions of the adrenal glands, and over- or under-secretion by the pituitary gland (Brussel and Irwin 1973, 49).

Postpartum depression • Often called the "four day blues," postpartum depression is experienced by many mothers a few days after the birth of a child. Childbirth can be an exhausting experience. The mother's body has been subjected to several months of significant stress. In addition many hormonal and metabolic changes take place. Immediately following the birth of the child there is joy and elation. There are visits from happy friends and family. However, as soon as the first flash of excitement passes and exhaustion sets in, it is very common for the new mother to experience a letdown and mild depression. This reaction is not abnormal and should be understood by family and friends. With a little understanding and support most women are themselves again in a few days. However, in some cases it can become prolonged and quite severe. A woman who does not come out of postpartum depression in a few days should receive professional care.

PSYCHOLOGICAL CAUSES

While there are many psychological causes of depression, we believe that most of them fall under one of the following categories: loss, anger, guilt, and faulty thinking.

Loss • Norman Wright says, "The common thread that underlies much of depression is loss" (Wright 1977, 69). Minirth and Meier state, "Probably the most common stress that precipitates a depression is suffering a significant loss" (Minirth and Meier 1978, 98). There are many types of losses that can lead to depression. These include the loss of a loved one, the loss of a job, the loss of some significant object, or the loss of self-esteem. Any loss that is significant to the person involved, even if it seems insignificant to others, can lead to depression. Job, in the Bible, is an example of depression brought on by loss—read Job 3 to see how he expressed his reactions.

Anger • Several writers on depression suggest that depression usually involves repressed anger (Kennedy et al.). Loss and repressed anger are often related to each other. Minirth and Meier explain,

> *Whenever we suffer a significant loss of any kind, we go through modified grief reaction.... We feel some anger, whether we are aware of it or not. If that anger is repressed it will lead to depression (Minirth and Meier 1978, 99).*

For example, a Christian husband experiences the loss of a wife. The husband may feel some anger toward God for not letting his wife live. The husband also feels it is wrong to be angry at God, so he represses the anger rather than express it. This repressed anger is likely to lead to depression. When a person loses anything there is a tendency to blame others and be angry with them. When that anger is repressed rather than dealt with in a responsible way, depression often results.

Guilt • We have already distinguished between true and false guilt. Either type of guilt can cause depression. While depression is an abnormal reaction to false guilt, it is a normal reaction to true guilt. We pointed out at the beginning of this chapter that depression is a symptom of another problem. True guilt is a real problem. Humans are sinners who are guilty before God. While God has made provision for sin, and forgiveness is freely offered, the fact of guilt is not removed. People who do not deal with their sin experience guilt. This is real guilt and can lead to depression, especially for Christians. Unconfessed sin and secret sins are a major cause of depression among Christians.

Faulty thinking • Faulty thought processes can also be a major source of depression. False guilt involves faulty thinking. Those who experience guilt over a matter that should not produce guilt are practicing faulty thinking. Faulty thinking may involve setting unrealistic goals and then feeling depressed when they are not achieved. Faulty thinking may involve having unrealistic expectations about something like marriage or a job, and feeling depressed because it is not as expected. Basically, faulty thinking involves distorting reality in some way. Some psychologists believe that all psychologically caused depression is ultimately the result of faulty thinking (Hauch 1973). It should be noted, however, that faulty thinking may also be a result of depression.

CONSEQUENCES OF DEPRESSION

There are many consequences of depression. Depressed people, of course, suffer the gloom and despair of depression. Job performance and relationships with friends and family are affected. The daily life of the depressed and of those around them is adversely affected. However, the most serious consequence of depression, at least in the immediate sense, is that depressed people have a tendency to self-injury. As Professor Eugene Kennedy explains in his book *On Becoming a Counselor*, "One of the chief but not well-understood traits found in depressed persons is their capacity for hurting themselves" (Kennedy 1977, 162). He points out that depressed persons are more accident-prone and get sick more often than the general public. Kennedy believes some depressed persons often allow themselves to get ill or injured in order to receive sympathy. He thinks other depressed people get ill or injured as a form of self-punishment. Still others may do so as a way of getting back at others. Whatever the reasons for this tendency, the counselor needs to be aware of it. Part of any ministry to the depressed needs to include concern for their immediate safety.

The most extreme form of this tendency toward hurting oneself is suicide. As pointed out earlier, depression is the leading cause of suicide. Suicide is discussed in the next chapter; however, at this point it is important to recognize that suicide is often a consequence of depression and thus depression should be taken seriously. Because the various consequences of depression are serious for both the depressed persons and those around them, we need to be prepared to minister to those who suffer from this problem.

COUNSELING THE DEPRESSED

This extended discussion of the symptoms and causes of depression should provide a basic understanding of the nature of depression so that we may minister to those suffering from it. Further reading in this area is of course desirable.

In counseling with depressed persons the seven basic steps of Reality Therapy (chapter 4) may be utilized. One of the basic characteristics of an effective counselor discussed in chapter 3 is flexibility. We do not need to apply these seven steps in a rigid fashion, but can modify them as the situation requires.

While we always need to be interested in the counselee, Norman Wright points out that it is especially important "that rapport is established with a depressed person" (Wright 1977, 76). Depressed people need a great deal of support and acceptance. This can grow out of a healing relationship. Empathy and warmth are especially important in our involvement with depressed persons. They must be assured of God's love and acceptance. Wright suggests the following passages of Scripture as helpful at this point: Isaiah 40:28-31; 42:3; 43:1-4; Philippians 4:4-9 (Wright 1977, 76).

The next step is to *examine behavior* and thoughts for causes of the depression. We might ask, "What have you been doing or thinking that might be causing your depression?" Quite frequently people are aware of the source of their depression. When the person is not able to suggest a cause for his or her depression, we need to explore some possibilities with the counselee. A good place to begin is with physical causes. We may inquire about how the counselee is feeling and about particular life functions. For instance, after learning or observing that a person has a saddened mood, we would appropriately ask "How are you sleeping?" and "How is your appetite?" The difference between discouragement and depression in a medical sense is that depression, as discussed earlier, involves a syndrome of changes in life functions. Accordingly we would go on to inquire about energy or ambition levels and the person's efficiency or ability to concentrate. We should be sensitive to possible drug or alcohol use.

When interviewing a depressed person, it is always important to inquire about despairing thoughts: "Do you ever feel like giving up?" or "Does it seem like life isn't worth the effort?" When receiving yes responses to such questions, we should take them seriously. (Please see chapter 10 on suicide.)

When answers to the previous questions form a pattern of affirmative responses showing that there are changes in sleep, a loss of ambition, and a decreased ability to concentrate, in addition to a depressed mood, we begin to think of the person as depressed. If these symptoms are severe enough to adversely affect daily functioning or if they persist, the person should be encouraged to seek professional counsel.

It is important to remember that depression itself is an illness and when it becomes severe it can be very serious. It is also important to realize that, for some, depressive illness is biochemical in nature and therefore will require antidepressant medication to facilitate proper functioning of nerve endings in the brain. Such diagnosis requires a professional opinion and if medication is needed, the treatment must be managed by a physician.

The Bible teaches that Christians are responsible for the care of their bodies (Rom. 12:1; 1 Cor. 6:12-20; 1 Tim. 5:23). Our bodies are a stewardship from God (Gen. 1:26-28). We need to maintain a proper diet and get adequate exercise and sufficient rest. There are psychological, as well as physical, costs to abusing our bodies. On the other hand, proper diet, exercise, and rest will pay rich dividends, both psychologically and physically.

If there do not seem to be any physical causes for the depression, then the counselor and counselee need to explore for precipitating events. A list of the types of events that may bring on depression is given in Table 9-1. We might ask the counselee if any of the events listed have occurred in the past year. People's depression may very well result from events in their lives even when they do not see the connection. We should be particularly sensitive to losses in the person's life or to events that might lead to resentment or repressed anger. When events or circumstances that might have precipitated the depression have been discovered, the person's reactions to the events or circumstances need to be evaluated.

TABLE 9-1

THE HOLMES-RAHE SOCIAL READUSTMENT RATING
SCALE (Holmes and Rahe 1963, 2:213-18)

EVENTS	SCALE OF IMPACT
Death of a spouse	100
Divorce	73
Marital separation	65
Jail term	63
Death of close family member	63
Personal injury or illness	53
Marriage	50
Fired at work	47
Marital reconciliation	45
Retirement	45
Change in health of family member	44
Pregnancy	40
Sex difficulties	39
Gain of new family member	39
Business readjustment	39
Change in financial state	38
Death of close friend	37
Change to different line of work	36
Change in number of arguments with spouse	35
Mortgage over $10,000 *(Today $30,000 might be a better figure.)*	31
Foreclosure of mortgage or loan	30
Change in responsibilities at work	29
Son or daughter leaving home	29
Trouble with in-laws	29
Outstanding personal achievement	28
Wife begins or stops work	26
Begin or end school	26
Change in living conditions	25
Revision of personal habits	24
Trouble with boss	23
Change in work hours or conditions	20
Change in residence	20
Change in schools	20

EVENTS	SCALE OF IMPACT
Change in recreation	19
Change in church activities	19
Change in social activities	18
Mortgage or loan less than $10,000 ($20,000 today)	17
Change in sleeping habits	16
Change in number of family get-togethers	15
Change in eating habits	15
Vacation	13
Christmas	12
Minor violations of the law	11

The relative impact of each of these events is indicated. The effect of these events is cumulative. If more than one of these events has taken place in the life of a person in the past year, the point value of each event should be totaled up. While any one of these events, especially the first six, can bring on depression, research with this test indicates that persons with events totaling 200 or more points have a significant increase in psychiatric disorders, especially depression (Minirth and Meier 1978, 118).

The extent of depression can vary from slight to moderate to severe. A person who is slightly depressed may show several of the signs and symptoms described earlier but have little difficulty with functioning at normal tasks. When normal functioning is impaired, a person is moderately depressed. At this point the consequences of depression become more serious with the increased possibility of secondary effects including accidents, irritability, and decreased efficiency on the job. When a person is severely depressed normal functioning becomes impossible. *Evaluation* of behavior should include an assessment of the degree of depression. Depression that progresses to moderate or severe is beyond the capabilities of lay counselors. Such persons should be referred to a physician or another qualified professional.

While many events and circumstances can lead to depression, it is the individual's reaction that determines the severity and length of the depression. For example, a man may lose his wife in an accident. This is obviously a sad event and grief is a normal reaction. The person can say to himself, "This is a great loss and I will have some difficult days ahead, but I know she would want me to go on with life and I will." On the other hand, the person might say, "This is a great loss and now life has no purpose; I have nothing to live for." In the first instance the person will probably go through a normal grief process and return to normal functioning. In the second instance the person will probably go into a state of depression. It is how a person reacts to an event that is important.

We need to help a depressed counselee evaluate his or her reaction to a life situation. It is not so much the situation as it is the reactions to that situation that is responsible for depression. At this point it may be appropriate for us and the counselee to evaluate reactions in light of Scripture. The Bible teaches us the appropriate way to deal with loss, anger, and guilt (see Table 5-1 in chapter 5).

When the counselee's behavior, reactions, and thinking have been evaluated, a *plan of action* needs to be formulated. The principles and steps set forth in the chapter on guidance counseling (chapter 6) should be utilized in developing a plan of action.

In addition to the specific plans made for dealing with the causes of depression, Wright offers a list of specific suggestions that may be offered to a depressed person:

1. *Try to keep up your daily routine.*
2. *Try to get out of the house, even for very short*

periods of time.

3. *Try to see family members and friends as much as possible but for very short periods of time.*
4. *Try to engage in deliberate physical activity; this is very important for overcoming depression.*
5. *Try to write a note to people if it is too difficult to talk with them.*
6. *Try to tell your family and friends that scolding and criticism is not helpful, you need their support and encouragement.*
7. *Try to let your family know what you are feeling.*
8. *Try to remember that even severe depressions usually end.*
9. *Try to find a person you trust, to whom you can complain and express your anger.*
10. *Try to resume normal eating and sleeping habits* (Wright 1977, 77-78).

When working with a depressed person, it is very important to make plans realistic and attainable. The plan should respect this fact and therefore be made up of small, easily accomplished steps.* "One day at a time" is a valuable slogan; it summarizes Jesus' teaching when He said, *Therefore do not worry about tomorrow, for tomorrow will worry about itself. Each day has enough trouble of its own (Matt. 6:34).* It is important for the depressed person to avoid failure and experience success. Scripture and prayer need to play an important part in the planning process.

When a viable plan has been made, the depressed person must express *commitment to the plan.* This step is particularly critical in counseling with the depressed

---

*We need to keep in mind that depression is a mechanism for withdrawing from life temporarily because either circumstances or inner problems are overwhelming.

who may be dependent and will agree to anything. It is important that a counselee decide on the plan and give verbal assent. When dealing with a Christian counselee, prayer should be a basic part of the commitment process. The individual needs to make the commitment to God.

While we need to encourage and support a depressed person, we must *never accept excuses* for failure. While it is important for any counselee to accept responsibility, it is essential for a depressed person. If the plan turns out to be unrealistic, it should be revised. If it is still viable, have the counselee recommit himself or herself to it and try again.

Accepting a counselee's excuses will only make the person more dependent and less responsible, and it is likely to deepen the depression. By not accepting his excuses, we are telling him we have confidence in him, that we know he can do it.

We do not accept excuses, but we *do not give punishment* either. The last thing a depressed person needs is scolding and nagging. The depressed person needs support and encouragement. We need to treat depressed persons as responsible beings if we expect them to act like responsible beings.

Peter committed himself to not denying the Lord (John 13:36-37). Peter then failed to live up to his commitment (John 18:25-27). When Jesus met Peter again, He did not condemn or punish him, but asked for a recommitment (John 21:15-17). Jesus models effective counseling for us.

In dealing with severely depressed persons, or persons who do not respond to counseling, a counselor should not hesitate to refer that person to someone else.

Depression, in the sense of a discouraged mood, is usually related to circumstances and is therefore transient. When the situation changes, the person's mood will improve. On the other hand, depression as a syndrome, extending beyond circumstances or a precipitating event, is a significant problem. It may either be the sign of a disease or a medical illness in itself. Accordingly a depressed person needs to be taken seriously. Loving concern may be the basis for a healing relationship, or it may provide the motivation for a referral to a helping professional.

DISCUSSION QUESTIONS

1. Can a Spirit-filled Christian ever experience depression? Why?
2. Why do women seek help for depression more often than men? What does this say to Christians about reaching out to men who are depressed?
3. Have you ever been depressed? What were the symptoms? Can you relate your experience to the discussion in this chapter?
4. How large a role does faulty thinking play in depression? Why?
5. Why is it important to refer persons who suffer severe or prolonged depression?

SUGGESTED READING

Brussel, James A. and Irwin, Theodore. *Understanding and Overcoming Depression*. New York: Hawthorne Books, 1973. A secular introduction to the problem of depression. Contains a good chapter on prevention.

Hauch, Paul A. *Overcoming Depression*. Philadelphia: Westminster, 1973. A cognitive approach to overcoming depression. This book deals with faulty thinking and how to correct it; valuable reading.

LaHaye, Tim. *How to Win Over Depression*. Grand Rapids: Zondervan, 1974. A helpful book that lay persons can easily comprehend. However many professional therapists find LaHaye somewhat simplistic.

Minirth, Frank B. and Meier, Paul D. *Happiness Is a Choice*. Grand Rapids: Baker, 1978. A work by two Christian psychiatrists on both the physical and psychological causes of depression. A medical approach to the physical causes and a cognitive approach to the psychological causes.

Trobisch, Walter. *Love Yourself: Self-acceptance and Depression*. Downers Grove, Ill.: InterVarsity, 1976. A book that considers self-image and how it relates to depression. Contains an excellent discussion, from a Christian perspective, of dealing with a poor self-image.

CHAPTER TEN

Suicide

Mrs. Woodrum, a widow of fifty-five, early one morning jumped to her death from her twelfth-floor apartment on Chicago's north side. Just before she jumped, she saw the janitor working on the balcony across the court in the next wing of the building. Mrs. Woodrum waved to him and smiled. He smiled and waved back. When he turned his back, she jumped.

On her orderly desk, Mrs. Woodrum left this note: "I can't stand one more day of this loneliness. No sound from my telephone. No mail in my box. No friends." Mrs. Jenkins, another widow who lived on the same floor of the large city apartment building, told reporters, "I wish I had known she was lonely; I could have called on her. We could have been friends" (Grunlan and Mayers 1979, 189).

Between 27,000 and 30,000 Americans commit suicide each year.* It is the tenth-ranking cause of death in this

---

*Most experts concede these figures are low because many suicides are listed as accidents to protect the families of the deceased.

country. While more than twice as many females as males attempt suicide, almost three times as many males as females successfully commit suicide. Single persons are more likely to commit suicide than married persons. The widowed and the divorced have the highest rate. Chemically dependent people are more likely than the general population to commit suicide. Suicide is 30 percent more frequent than murder in this country (Slovic et al. 1980. 44).

Suicide is the second leading cause of death among teenagers according to *U.S. News and World Report* (November 12, 1984). In this age range almost four times as many males as females successfully commit suicide even though there are more female attempts. Among young adults, 20-24 years of age, suicide is the third leading cause of death behind accidents and cancer. College students are more likely to commit suicide than non-students of the same age.

The major means of suicide listed in their order of frequency are:

1. Firearms
2. Hanging and strangulation
3. Sleeping pills or other drugs
4. Gas, including exhaust fumes
5. Poisons
6. Drowning
7. Cutting or piercing

DETECTING SUICIDAL POTENTIAL

How do we determine if a person is going to commit suicide or not? Mrs. Jenkins would have been glad to befriend Mrs. Woodrum if she had known she needed help. Each of us would be willing to reach out and help a person who was considering suicide. The question is, how do we know if suicide is being contemplated? As Christians we place a high value on human life and we seek every opportunity to preserve it. Several types of clues are given by people who are considering suicide.

VERBAL CLUES

An individual may give direct verbal clues. That is, he may say he is going to take his life. There is a false popular belief that a person who talks about suicide will not do it. The fact is that most people who commit suicide have told someone in advance. If an individual tells us that he or she is planning suicide, we need to take him or her seriously.

A person may also give indirect verbal clues. That is, he may allude to not being around anymore, life not being worth living, or some other such comments. Anyone who seems to be hinting at suicide should be asked about it directly.

If a person talks of suicide, it is often appropriate to ask him how he would do it. The more detailed the plan, especially if the means are readily available, the more important immediate intervention becomes. If you believe an individual is suicidal, tell him you are concerned about his plan and that you are going to tell a spouse, parents, children, or other concerned persons. You may also make a professional referral as you suggest the person get help.

BEHAVIORAL CLUES

Sudden, unexplained changes in behavior are often a clue to some problem. The types of behaviors that might indicate a potential suicide include the person who begins to put his affairs in order for no apparent reason. Attention to wills, insurance, and valuables may indicate a concern with death. Another clue is sudden elation in a person who has been quite depressed. People do not normally emerge suddenly from a deep depression; recovery is gradual. However, the person who has found the ultimate solution to his or her problem may suddenly feel elated. One who begins cutting off himself or herself from friends and loved ones may be preparing for a permanent departure. Behavior can often be a clue to what is happening inside a person.

SITUATIONAL CLUES

Certain situations have great potential for bringing on suicidal tendencies. Crises or stress beyond a person's ability to handle may bring on suicide. Crises such as the death of a loved one, the loss of a job, a serious illness or accident, an arrest, or a divorce can lead to suicide. However, it is not only negative crises that can lead to suicide; positive crises such as a promotion or graduation may also lead to suicide. Stress is a significant precipitating factor in suicide. The likelihood of suicide increases with the intensity of the stress. What may be a stressful situation for one person may not be for another. It is the effect a situation has on the particular individual involved that must be considered.

PSYCHOLOGICAL CLUES

Certain psychological states are associated with suicide. The most common is depression. As pointed out in the previous chapter, depression is the leading cause of suicide. Other psychological clues include hopelessness, disorientation, and complaining. The sudden appearance of deviant behavior may also be a clue. Persons whose emotional states change suddenly and radically are generally giving evidence of some sort of psychological problems. Such persons may act irresponsibly. We need to be sensitive to people's psychological states as indicators of potential suicide.

DEMOGRAPHIC CLUES

Demographic clues are related to population characteristics. Certain segments of the population are more prone to suicide. When the above clues are observed in members of these segments of the population, we need to be even more sensitive to them.

We have already pointed out that males are about three times as likely to commit suicide than are females. We have seen that divorced and widowed persons are higher than average risks. The young and the aged are greater risks than the middle aged. Students are also a greater risk. Individuals with unstable lifestyles and the drug dependent also have greater potential for suicide. Statistically, persons in these segments of the population have the highest suicide rates.

SUICIDE INTERVENTION

The average lay counselor is usually not competent to counsel with suicidal persons. A suicidal person, that is a person who is seriously considering taking his or her own life, usually needs professional help. Because the consequences of mishandling a suicidal person are fatal, it is generally recommended that lay counselors refer suicidal persons (see chapter 13 for information on making referrals).

However, while lay persons may not be as effective as professional counselors in helping suicidal persons, research indicates that they are just as effective as professional counselors in suicide intervention. Suicide intervention means keeping suicidal persons from taking their lives. Paul Pretzel, a psychologist with vast experience in suicide prevention, suggests there are six levels of suicide intervention (Pretzel 1972, 108-16). The counselor's responsibility differs at each level.

FIRST LEVEL:
PHYSICAL INTERVENTION

At this level the suicidal person has already either completed the suicidal act or is in the process of carrying it out. If the person has already taken action—cut the wrists, swallowed the pills, jumped from the window, etc.—then one needs to send for medical assistance and to stabilize the person medically—i.e., stop the bleeding, cut the rope from the neck, start artificial respiration, etc. If the person has already committed the act, concern at that point focuses on his or her physical condition.

If the person is involved in attempting suicide, that is, cutting his wrists, swallowing the pills, etc., then one needs to physically stop the action if possible. One needs to be concerned for personal safety as well as the safety of the suicidal person. If one can safely intervene in the suicide attempt, this should be the first course of action. Again, the main concern is with getting medical assistance and stabilizing the person medically.

SECOND LEVEL:
PSYCHOLOGICAL INTERVENTION

At this level the person has clearly determined to commit suicide and has the means (gun, pills, knife, etc.) available but has not yet begun to take action. The number one rule at this level of intervention is not to leave the suicidal person alone. In this state he may feel abandoned and commit the act. A counselor on the phone with a person at this level should not hang up to go be with him or her. One should either stay on the phone and send someone else (the police if no one else is available) or have someone else take over the phone while the counselor goes over.

The next step is to try to confiscate the means of suicide, if possible, or try to get the person to dispose of it. The first concern is with the person's physical safety. One should not attempt to confiscate the means of suicide if it appears that this will push the person into acting. While following the suggestions below the counselor might make continual attempts to get the person to dispose of the means of suicide.

A counselor should try to talk through alternatives with a suicidal person at this level. An attempt needs to be made to help the person see that the situation is not hopeless but that there are alternatives. If a suicidal person can find some source of hope, he or she may give up the decision to take his or her life. The second principle of guidance counseling, delineating the options (see chapter 6), may be utilized here. One should explore every option, no matter how farfetched, if it keeps the person talking. At this point the viability of an option is not as important as its effect on the suicidal person. Once a person has given up the decision to commit suicide, more realistic options can be explored in follow-up counseling.

A word of warning must be given about dealing with persons at this level. The counselor should not try to call a bluff or dare the person. Reverse psychology will backfire. Calling the person's bluff by daring him to act may very well drive him to act. It is important to play it straight in dealing with suicidal persons.

THIRD LEVEL: STRESS OR SITUATION INTERVENTION

At this level the person is under unmanageable stress

or in a situation where suicide is being considered as an option. The seven steps of Reality Therapy may be used to help the person develop and mobilize a plan of action to reduce stress and handle the situation. At this level, if we are unable to help the person to overcome his suicidal ideas, we should not hesitate to refer the person to other sources of help.

The most important aspect of intervention is moving the person away from suicide as an option and helping him develop strategies for coping. Spiritual resources may be introduced at this level of intervention. Faith can play an important part in relieving stress. We can help a counselee utilize the resources of faith. Counselees who are Christians should be reminded of the importance of prayer and of bringing their problems to God. With counselees who do not have a personal faith, counselors can share their own faith and offer an opportunity to respond. A word of caution at this point needs to be made. We should not present our faith as a crutch for crises. Rather, it should be presented as a total way of life that enables one to deal with crises. A faith accepted as a crutch will be discarded when the crisis is over, but a faith that is accepted as a way of life will continue.

FOURTH LEVEL: SUPPORTING INTERNAL COPING MECHANISMS

At this level the person is under great stress or in a difficult situation but has not yet seriously considered suicide. Intervention consists of supporting an individual's internal coping mechanisms so that suicide never becomes a serious option. An important aspect of coping is self-acceptance or a good self-image. We also need to help people accept situations they cannot change such as a death or divorce. The discussions on guidance counseling (chapter 6) and crisis counseling (chapter 7) may be useful at this point.

When dealing with Christian counselees, we need to help them realize that they are important and worthwhile. A passage of Scripture that concerns this issue is Ephesians 1:3-14. Verse 3 tells us that as Christians we have been blessed *with every spiritual blessing in Christ.* Verse 4 says we have been chosen before the foundations of the earth. God has picked us out, we are special. Verse 5 teaches we have been adopted as the children of God. We are children of the King! We are somebody! Verse 6 says God has *freely* (NIV) or *lavishly* (NASB) given us His grace. Verse 7 tells us we have forgiveness for sin. There is no more need for self-condemnation and guilt. Verses 8 to 10 tell us God has shared with us His plan for the ages. We are the confidants of God. We are somebody! Verses 11 and 12 again remind us that we are a chosen people. Verse 13 teaches we have the seal of God, and verse 14 declares that we have an inheritance waiting for us. We are heirs! In Christ we are somebody. As Christian counselors we need to share this good news.

FIFTH LEVEL: REDUCING STRESS

The emphasis of the fifth level changes from intervention to prevention. We should try to recognize stressful situations before they become unmanageable so that we may develop a plan of action to reduce stress. Also this level involves recognizing potentially suicidal conditions and dealing with them. At this level we seek to reduce stress and help the counselee adjust to situations so that he never gets to level three. The techniques of guidance and crisis counseling can be used as well as the Christian resources of the Word and prayer.

SIXTH LEVEL:
PRIMARY PREVENTION

This level involves the maintenance of normal social support and services for persons who are most susceptible to suicide such as students, the elderly, the widowed, and divorced. Take the case of Mrs. Woodrum at the beginning of the chapter. If she had received normal social support, she would not have contemplated suicide. We need to be sensitive to those around us who may be prone to suicide and be ready to reach out to them. It is at the fifth and sixth levels that the local church, as a body, can and should become involved. The church is uniquely equipped to function as a support group.

MISTAKES TO AVOID

Paul Pretzel suggests that there are at least three types of mistakes that need to be avoided when dealing with suicidal persons (Pretzel 1972, 108-16).

OVERREACTION

It is very easy for a counselor to overreact to a suicidal situation. There are three major types of overreactions. One is panic. It is very important to remain calm. If we panic, the suicidal person may also panic and commit the act. If the act has already been committed and we panic, the person may bleed or choke to death, but if the counselor remains calm, he or she might save a life.

Anger is another overreaction to suicide. Anger may be a cover for fear or it may indicate our resentment toward the person. In any case, we should not get angry with a suicidal person. Another overreaction is to use unnecessary physical intervention. If at all possible, we should get the person himself to dispose of the means of suicide. Physical intervention should be a last resort.

UNDERREACTION

It is possible to underreact as well as overreact. The most common type of underreaction is not taking a suicide threat seriously. People who threaten suicide commit suicide. Almost all suicide victims tell someone before they do it. We need to take the threat of suicide seriously.

Another underreaction is to appear so impassive that no empathy or understanding is communicated. In an attempt to be calm it is possible to come across cold. We need to be involved with the person and to communicate that involvement.

INAPPROPRIATE RESPONSES

There are two significant forms of inappropriate responses that often occur in suicide counseling. The first is avoiding the subject of suicide. The issue of suicide needs to be raised and dealt with. Ignoring it will not make it go away. It is important to face the issue of suicide head on.

The second inappropriate response is to discuss the situation and suicide on an intellectual level or in an academic way. The discussion needs to be personal. The issue needs to be dealt with at the personal level. We need to be sure that we discuss the issue of suicide and that we do so in a personal way.

SUMMARY

Suicide is a common response to stress and depression. Individuals, as well as congregations, need to be prepared to minister to those who are considering suicide as a means of dealing with their problems. We need to be reaching out to people before they even get to that point. We need to recognize suicide for the threat it is and be prepared to minister at all six levels discussed.

DISCUSSION QUESTIONS

1. *Do you know anyone who ever attempted or committed suicide? Can you relate that experience to the discussion in this chapter? How?*
2. *If someone hears an acquaintance who is believed to be stable talk about ending his life, should that person take the talk seriously or dismiss it as idle chatter? Why? What would you do?*
3. *Would a Christian attempt suicide? Why?*
4. *What are the most important things to remember when dealing with a suicidal person?*

SUGGESTED READING

Pretzel, Paul. *Understanding and Counseling the Suicidal Person.* Nashville: Abingdon, 1972. A comprehensive study of suicide. Some valuable discussions on the prevention of suicide.

Lum, Doman. *Responding to Suicidal Crisis.* Grand Rapids: Eerdmans, 1974. A discussion of suicide prevention as a form of crisis intervention. This book is geared to pastors and lay persons working in the local church.

Schneidman, Edwin and Farberow, Norman L., eds. *Clues to Suicide.* New York: McGraw-Hill, 1957. A collection of articles on suicide. The articles center around demographic and situational clues to suicide.

Stengel, Erwin. *Suicide and Attempted Suicide.* 2nd ed. New York: Pelican, 1969. A good discussion of the distinction between suicide and real attempts to commit suicide as opposed to those attempts that are cries for help and not attempts to die.

CHAPTER ELEVEN

Marriage and Family Counseling

With their wedding date still a few months off, Fred breaks his engagement to Sue because he feels she is too immature to develop a meaningful relationship. Two weeks later Sue meets Ralph who is 38, twenty years her senior. Ralph has been married twice before, his last wife divorcing him while he was in a state mental hospital for observation of aggressive tendencies (wife beating). Sue's parents are against her marrying Ralph to whom she became engaged after only six weeks. The parents are evangelical Christians and Sue has been raised in a Christian home and has made a profession of faith while Ralph was baptized as an infant but has not involved himself with a church since he was a child. Sue's parents also want Sue to go to college and are concerned that Ralph is a high school dropout. Sue's parents have come to you as a Christian counselor. They would like you to talk with Sue about her relationship with Ralph.

Carl and Sally have been married for three years and find that they are arguing more and more. Communication seems to have completely broken down. As Sally describes it, they seem to talk at each other rather than to each other. They both feel that they love each other and both want their marriage to work, but they do not know what to do. They have come to you for some advice. They want help in developing a better relationship.

George and Edna have been married for twenty-six years and have three children, the youngest of whom will be leaving for college in a couple of months. The older children are married. George suffered a mild heart attack last year, and his doctor has restricted his activities. George had to turn down another firm's job offer that would have meant a major advance in his career. Edna had three years of college before they were married and now that their youngest child is leaving for college she wants to start attending classes at a local branch of the state university to work toward a teaching degree. George is upset by this because he feels he earns enough money to support the family and because his aged mother who was just widowed needs a place to live. George would like to bring her to his home and have his wife stay home and care for her. This has led to serious tension in their relationship. They come to you for help in working through their problems.

Marriage and family counseling deals with those problems related to beginning and maintaining a family. Charles Stewart, a professor of pastoral counseling, defines marriage and family counseling as "a process in which a counselor helps persons, couples, or families to make plans and to solve problems in the area of courtship, marriage, and family relations" (Stewart 1970, 21). Based on this definition marriage and family counseling may be divided into three basic areas: premarital counseling, marriage counseling, and family counseling. Before examining each of these areas separately, we would like to lay a foundation for marriage and family counseling.

FOUNDATIONS FOR MARRIAGE: ROOTS OF RELATIONSHIPS

Preparation for marriage begins before either individual is self-conscious; in fact, every marriage has its roots in the soil of the preceding generations. The family is a system and any attempt to understand the family, or the marriages that issue from it, needs to begin with an awareness of the rules that govern the system.

What do we mean by the term *system*? We are all acquainted with systems in other areas, but perhaps have not applied the idea to people. For instance, a tree or plant is a system. It has roots, a trunk, branches, leaves, and blossoms. The life of that organic system is governed by rules. Some of the rules, like the need for light and water, are basic and apply to all plant systems. Others are more specialized and apply to different kinds of plants. When the rules are met the plant flourishes; when the plant is uprooted, inadequately watered, receives too little or too much light, or is too crowded it will become unhealthy and perhaps bear no flowers or fruit. It is helpful in premarital counseling as well as in marriage and family counseling, to ask, where are these individuals coming from? What are their roots and what formative rules govern their growth? Some persons have grown up in families where decision making is the task of one person who commands or demands compliance by other family members; others have developed an inner set of growth rules in a family where the mother and father jointly make decisions and where the parents ask the children to participate in the process. Decision making is an important part of each family system. Conflict often develops when a person from one type of system marries a person who was raised in a different system.

Other important aspects of family systems involve finances, discipline, time, communication—including

what can be talked about, in what manner and to whom
—expression of affection through word and touch, as
well as allowing for fear and anger. Family systems also
extend to relationships with other families and society at
large. Every family has its own rules in each of these
areas, and every individual comes to marriage with his
or her roots of relationships well established. Many people are not conscious of this rootage, taking their own
ways of being and doing for granted. They presume that
everyone else is governed by the same (or very similar)
internalized rules. The lay counselor will be better prepared to understand the backgrounds of people who
come for help having made an effort to understand his or
her own background.

Counselors should be conscious that all families have
rules that function in a systematic way and that these
rules come from the larger family systems where an individual has his roots and his formative influences. This
awareness will improve the overall process of marriage
and family counseling.

PREMARITAL COUNSELING

Marriage, especially in its beginnings, is very stressful. In fact, on life-change scales it has been rated as one
of life's most stressful experiences (see Table 9-1). Since
marriage is such a significant life change, it is an oppor-
tune time for each prospective husband and wife to experience the support and the insight of an effective counseling relationship.

In general, a couple should receive premarital counseling from the pastor who will perform the marriage or
from a qualified marriage counselor. However, there
may be times when an individual or a couple will not go
to a pastor or professional counselor, for one reason or
another, but they will talk with a fellow Christian. In

those situations lay counselors need to be available. Also, some churches are organizing trained lay counselors to do some premarital counseling under the supervision of a pastor. In either case, we need to have some basic guidelines for premarital counseling.

SOCIOLOGICAL FACTORS

Marriage is a social arrangement. As noted earlier, each person brings a unique sociological background to the marriage. Research has revealed some sociological factors associated with successful marriages and others associated with unsuccessful marriages.* There are of course exceptions to these findings; yet it is important to acknowledge that they are just that, exceptions. Statistically these factors are able to help us predict the chances of success or failure for marriages.

William Stephens, a sociologist, analyzed the research available on the sociological factors and isolated seventeen sociological factors for predicting marital success (Stephens 1970, 189-99). We will look at them in descending order of predictiveness; that is, the first one is statistically the strongest predictor and the last one is the statistically weakest.

1. *Age at marriage.* The research findings on the relationship between age and marriage all indicate that the younger the parties are, the less successful the marriage. The divorce rates are highest when either the girl is under eighteen or the boy under twenty.
2. *Length of acquaintanceship.* All of the studies

---

*While researchers use many different types of measures of success, the most common is whether or not a couple is still married after five years. Most divorces take place in the first four years of marriage.

agree that the longer a couple has known each other before the wedding the more successful the marriage. Couples who have known each other less than a year have higher than average divorce rates.

3. *Premarital pregnancy.* Half of all marriages where the bride is pregnant end in divorce. If the bride is also a teenager, it is close to 70 percent. In Christian circles, there has been a tendency toward "shotgun" weddings. A forced solution often compounds the previous mistake.

4. *Religiosity.* The more religious a couple is, the more successful their marriage will be. The old saying, "Those who pray together, stay together," appears to be an accurate observation.

5. *Similarity of faith.* Mixed marriages (e.g., Protestant-Catholic, Catholic-Jewish) have higher divorce rates than same-faith marriages.

6. *Social class.* Contrary to what some may believe, all the studies clearly show that as income goes up, divorce goes down. Also, the larger the social class difference between a couple, the higher the divorce rate.

7. *Level of education.* The more years of education a couple has, the lower the divorce rate.

8. *Previous divorce.* Marriages involving divorced persons have higher divorce rates. The research indicates that divorced men are more likely to get a second divorce than divorced women.

9. *Divorced parents.* Persons with divorced parents have higher divorce rates than persons whose parents are still married. Men with divorced parents have higher divorce rates than women with divorced parents.

10. *Residence.* Persons living in rural areas have lower divorce rates than persons from urban

areas.

11. *Parental approval.* Couples who marry without parental approval have higher divorce rates than those who have the approval of their families.
12. *Sociability.* The more friends a person has, the better a marriage risk. "Loners" are poor marriage risks.
13. *Difference in age.* Couples with a difference of more than five years in their ages have higher divorce rates than those who are about the same age.
14. *Siblings.* Only children have higher divorce rates than persons with brothers and/or sisters.
15. *Relationship with parents.* Persons who do not get along with their parents have a higher divorce rate than those who do.
16. *Relationship with future spouse.* Couples who do not get along before marriage, do not get along after marriage.
17. *Mental health.* The better adjusted a person is, the more successful the marriage will be.

In premarital counseling, we do not necessarily use these sociological factors to discourage a couple from marrying. Rather, we use them to help them to better understand their relationship, and some of the potential pitfalls. In Reality Therapy, a major step in counseling is evaluating the situation. We need to help the couple face reality and then develop a responsible plan of action.

We also need to remember that many of these factors may be overcome. Young people will grow older. Non-religious persons can experience conversion. On the other hand, some of these factors cannot be changed. For instance, one cannot change the fact that his or her parents were divorced, but counseling can help a person understand the effect the parents' divorce had in his or her life so that the negative effects can be reduced.

INTERPERSONAL FACTORS

A very important aspect of premarital counseling is exploring the relationship between the couple. What is their relationship based on, infatuation or mature love? Table 11-1 presents a comparison of immature and mature love. The nature of true love is also described for us in 1 Corinthians 13:4-6. A relationship that is not based on mature love or *agape* love will not stand the test of time.

It is also important to examine the nature of the relationship. Many relationships between couples seeking marriage (and those already married) are unhealthy. An example of an unhealthy relationship is what some have called the parent-child syndrome. In this type of pairing one person comes to the relationship needing to be cared for (a "child"), and the other person comes with a great need to take care of him or her. The result is a marriage not of husband and wife, but of parent and child. This often leads to frustration, resentment, and severe marital conflict. Another unhealthy relationship is the neurotic pairing based on the psychological need to hurt and to be hurt.

We also need to examine the motives for the relationship. Some people marry out of pity, duty, or guilt. None of these is a sound basis for a marriage. Pity often leads to resentment, duty leads to drudgery, and guilt leads to hostility. The only basis for a healthy, maturing marriage is *agape* love.

MARITAL FACTORS

Premarital counseling needs to explore a number of areas related to the anticipated marriage. Sex, birth

TABLE 11-1

THE DIFFERENCE BETWEEN IMMATURE LOVE AND MATURE LOVE (Kelley 1969, 212-13)

IMMATURE LOVE	MATURE LOVE
1. *Love is born at first sight and will conquer all.*	1. *Love is a developing relationship and deepens with realistically shared experiences.*
2. *Love demands exclusive attention and devotion, and is jealous of outsiders.*	2. *Love is built upon self-acceptance and is shared unselfishly with others.*
3. *Love is characterized by exploitation and direct need gratification.*	3. *Love seeks to aid and strengthen the loved one without striving for recompense.*
4. *Love is built upon physical attraction and sexual gratification. Sex often dominates the relationship.*	4. *Love includes sexual satisfaction, but not to the exclusion of sharing in other areas of life.*
5. *Love is static and egocentric. Change is sought in the partner in order to satisfy one's own needs and desires.*	5. *Love is growing and developing reality. Love expands to include the growth and creativity of the loved one.*
6. *Love is romanticized. The couple does not face reality or is frightened by it.*	6. *Love enhances reality and makes the partners more complete and adequate persons.*
7. *Love is irresponsible and fails to consider the future consequences of today's action.*	7. *Love is responsible and gladly accepts the consequences of mutual involvement.*

control, and children are topics that need to be discussed. These important areas of marriage are a significant aspect of premarital counseling. Our attitudes and our expectations in these areas are closely related to our own developmental roots. Wandering into sexual experience through experimentation will not be a sufficient basis for mutual understanding and caring. Prior to marriage every couple should make opportunities to talk out their hopes and fears about their sexual relationship and their expectations with regard to having children. Couples have severe conflict when one wants to have children and the other does not. The partners sometimes enter marriage without reaching a mutually acceptable conclusion.

Sexual intimacy is emotional as well as physical; the couple who is limited to body experiences is cheated out of the fullness of an intimate relationship. General affection (a touch, a caress, a hug, or a kiss) is as important as genital affection, and it is important for a couple to talk out their needs, their satisfactions, and their discomforts.* Some persons come from families where such discussions are not allowed; they may, therefore, need a counselor's help in developing honest communication. This needed conversation may be initiated by reading and discussing a Scripture passage (e.g., the Song of Songs or 1 Cor. 7:1-7). It might also be helpful to ask some simple, direct questions regarding each person's expectations.

Concerning plans to have children, the lay counselor will want to be prepared to help a couple talk through

---

*In our counseling experience we have discovered that many couples have difficulty with sexual relations because there is little or no general affection. The foundation for a full and rich sexual experience begins at the breakfast table, not in the bedroom at the end of the day.

their thoughts and feelings with the intent of coming to a mutual conclusion. Below are twelve questions which may prove helpful:

1. Do you like children—not just cuddly infants but also cranky two-year-olds, curious eight-year-olds, and anxious teenagers?
2. Do you view parenthood as a burden or as an enriching experience?
3. Do you think your marriage will be strong enough for you to take on the responsibility of nurturing another person?
4. Are you willing to let go of your childhood and become an adult?
5. Can you give love without needing an equal amount in return?
6. Do you respond well to feelings of helplessness?
7. Do you have unrealistic expectations about parenthood? Do you believe, for example, that having a child will automatically ensure solace in your old age or save a troubled marriage?
8. Are you prepared for the profound changes parenthood will bring to your lifestyle in terms of money, time, and professional goals?
9. Are you prepared to work out the necessary compromises regarding child care (particularly in a dual-career situation)?
10. Are you prepared to let a child develop according to his or her bent, rather than according to your predetermined plan?
11. Are you prepared to depend more heavily on family and friends, as is usually necessary when a couple has a child?
12. Do you believe that it is consistent with God's leading in your life to have children at some point in the marriage?

Other areas that a couple needs to consider include

division of labor, budgeting, and in-law relationships. In the area of division of labor, each partner comes to a marriage with an idea of which tasks the husband should perform and which ones the wife should be responsible for. Generally, these ideas result from the person's upbringing. It is not so much a matter of one being right and the other wrong, but how to work out these differences. Another area which is a source of much contention in many marriages is finances. It is important in premarital counseling to help a couple think through a budget. The value of a budget is that it provides an opportunity for a couple to focus on and discuss their priorities and values. Also, we need to realize that a marriage does not bring only a husband and wife into a relationship but their families as well. This is another source of problems in marriage. We have all heard mother-in-law jokes and what makes most jokes funny is that they have a basis in fact. This is also an area that needs to be explored in premarital counseling. The biblical injunction to leave and cleave (Gen. 2:24) is well taken at this point.

SPIRITUAL FACTORS

From a Christian perspective, an important aspect of any marriage is the spiritual. A marriage that does not meet the biblical standards will never be all that it is possible for marriage to be.

As a starting point, are the couple biblically eligible to be married? Scripture is generally understood to teach that marriage between a believer and a nonbeliever is not condoned (2 Cor. 6:14-15). It is important for a couple to meet the biblical qualifications for marriage.

A good spiritual life provides the basis for a good marriage. There are two aspects to this. First, are both individuals maintaining a close walk with the Lord? Second, as a couple are they walking with the Lord? Are they having devotional times together? Are they praying together? Do they attend worship together? If they are not doing so before they are married, there is little reason to believe they will after they are married.

In premarital counseling it is useful to suggest some books for a couple to read together. Possible books are listed at the end of this chapter. If, during premarital counseling, serious problems are discovered, the couple should be urged to see a qualified minister or marriage counselor (see chapter 13 on making referrals).

MARRIAGE COUNSELING

The types of problems that may exist in a marriage are too numerous to list, much less discuss here. Some of the problems that arise in marriages are beyond the competency of most lay counselors and the best service is to refer the couple to a competent counselor. However, we should be able to help many couples if we are ready to do so. Of course the seven basic steps of Reality Therapy may be applied to most types of marital problems. In addition to these steps there are some principles that apply specifically to marriage counseling.

ALL MARRIAGES HAVE PROBLEMS

Christians should not be surprised to learn of problems in the marriages of church leaders, elders, deacons, Sunday school teachers, or anyone else. We need to realize that all marriages go through crises and problems. In some cases a couple may be able to work through the problem themselves; in other cases they may need outside help. Neither should we be shocked by the nature of the problems we may encounter. Since circumstances of modern life are complicated and stressful, human sinfulness manifests itself in many ways. If we show surprise or shock at what is revealed to us in counseling, counselees tend to cover up and our effectiveness will be diminished.

A MARRIAGE IS A SYSTEM

It is usually best to consider a marriage as a whole or a system. A change in one partner will affect the other. For example, if a couple has a parent-child relationship and we help the partner who is the "child" to mature and become less dependent, we take the "parent's" "child" away. The "parent" may need to become less domineering.

Another consideration in dealing with marriage as a system is to recognize and deal with differences. Reuel Howe says, "The differences between man and woman can be good" (Howe 1959, 119). God does not run an assembly line. He has made each of us unique individuals. Each partner needs to accept his or her own uniqueness as well as the other's uniqueness.

Differences between partners may exist in tastes or preferences, thought processes, habits, values, temperament, and many other areas. Six steps may help a couple to deal with differences. The first is awareness. A couple needs to be aware of their differences. The second step is acknowledgement. Couples often attempt to cover up their differences. This is usually unhelpful. The differences need to be talked about and dealt with in the open. The third step is acceptance. Couples need to accept differences (see our discussion on the acceptance of others in chapter 3). The fourth step is adaptation. Partners need to learn to adapt to each other. There needs to be some give-and-take in working out differences. The fifth step is appreciation. Each partner needs to express appreciation for the other, particularly for the other's uniqueness. The sixth step, admiration, is an outworking of the other five. The differences that attract people to each other in the first place may become irritants in marriage; dealing with the differences leads back to the admiration of courtship.

BOTH PARTNERS SHOULD BE INVOLVED

Marriage counselors are all but unanimous in saying that it is necessary to see both partners for the most effective counseling to take place. This need not mean seeing both partners together. There may be times when it is best to see each partner separately, especially in the initial stages of counseling. However, at some point we want to see them together. As we pointed out in the previous principle, a marriage is a system and we need to treat it as a whole.

Some professional marriage counselors refuse to see one partner alone. They insist on seeing both partners or they will not take a case. As Christian lay counselors we need to be ready to minister to anyone. It may be ideal to see both partners, but if one refuses to cooperate, we should work with the other as well as possible.

COMMUNICATION IS A KEY

Many marriage problems ultimately involve a communication breakdown. Andre Bustanoby, a Christian marriage and family counselor, says, "Almost without exception the couple with the troubled marriage is having a communication problem" (Wright 1977, 190). If we can help a couple to improve their communication, we have given them a tool for problem solving. Ten suggestions for marriage communications offered by Norman Wright are given in Table 11-2, Family Communications Guidelines.

TABLE 11-2

FAMILY COMMUNICATIONS GUIDELINES
(Wright 1977, 208-09)
Job 19:2; Proverbs 18:21; 25:11; James 3:8-10; 1 Peter 3:10

1. Be a ready listener and do not answer until the other person has finished talking (Prov. 18:13; James 1:19).
2. Be slow to speak. Think first. Don't be hasty in your words. Speak in such a way that the other person can understand and accept what you say (Prov. 15:23, 28; 21:23; 29:20; James 1:19).
3. Speak the truth always, but do it in love. Do not exaggerate (Eph. 4:15, 25; Col. 3:9).
4. Do not use silence to frustrate the other person. Explain why you are hesitant to talk at this time.
5. Do not become involved in quarrels. It is possible to disagree without quarreling (Prov. 17:14; 20:3; Rom. 13:13; Eph. 4:31).
6. Do not respond in anger. Use a soft and kind response (Prov. 14:29; 15:1; 25:15; 29:11; Eph. 4:26, 31).
7. When you are in the wrong, admit it and ask for forgiveness (James 5:16). When someone confesses to you, tell him you forgive him. Be sure it is *forgotten* and not brought up to the person (Prov. 17:9; Eph. 4:32; Col. 3:13; 1 Pet. 4:8).
8. Avoid nagging (Prov. 10:19; 17:9).
9. Do not blame or criticize the other but restore him, encourage him, and edify him (Rom. 14:13; Gal. 6:1; 1 Thess. 5:11). If someone verbally attacks, criticizes or blames you, do not respond in the same manner (Rom. 12:17, 21; 1 Pet. 2:23; 3:9).
10. Try to understand the other person's opinion.

Make allowances for differences. Be concerned about their interests (Phil. 2:1-4; Eph. 4:2).

Two normal, healthy persons cannot live together in an arrangement as intimate as marriage without ever disagreeing about something. It is rarely the disagreement that causes a problem, but, rather how it is handled. We would like to suggest some guidelines for handling disagreements or conflict in marriage:

1. It is all right to disagree. Conflict is normal. It is how it is handled that is important. If it is handled properly, it will be constructive and a stronger marriage will emerge.

2. Remember that the purpose is to resolve the disagreement, not win an argument. Marriage should be viewed as a cooperative arrangement, not a competitive one.

3. Compromise is not a dirty word. Generally neither party is completely right or wrong. Creative solutions involve give and take. See point two.

4. Stick to the issue at hand. Deal with the current issue. Do not bring up the past or side issues. Bringing in other issues can turn a small disagreement into a major conflict.

5. Fight fair. Do not try to trap the other person, use emotional responses, or otherwise use tactics that are designed to get your way rather than resolve the disagreement.

6. Listen to the other person. In any discussion in a marriage each partner should apply the ten points of effective listening given in chapter 3.

7. Include God. A couple should pray together about areas of disagreement. If both are Christians, both should want God's will.

8. Support the solution. When you arrive at a solution, both of you should support it even if it is not the position you initially wanted.

Even with the best communication skills, a couple's communication may still break down. In discussing intimacy, Howard Clinebell, a professor of pastoral counseling, and his wife, Charlotte, a marriage and family therapist, suggest several barriers which involve communication (Clinebell 1970, 44-60). The first barrier they suggest is *emotional immaturity*. Emotional immaturity in marriage can take different forms. It may involve having primary attachments with one's parents rather than one's spouse. It may involve egocentrism or self-centeredness. It may take the form of overdependence. It also generally involves a lack of responsibility.

Another barrier is the *fear of being hurt*. This is usually rooted in a lack of self-acceptance and/or emotional immaturity. The individual is afraid to disclose himself or herself or communicate openly for fear of being hurt, losing one's self-esteem, or losing the approval of others.

Low self-esteem is another barrier to communication. If a person does not value himself or herself, it will be difficult for that one to communicate openly. Low self-esteem leads to self-rejection and self-rejection leads to the rejection of the other. To avoid rejection both parties begin to avoid closeness and potential rejection.

Guilt, another barrier to communication, produces self-alienation. As one becomes alienated from self, one becomes alienated from others. Where guilt is real, there needs to be confession, forgiveness, and reconciliation both with God and the partner. Where there is false guilt (see chapter 2), there needs to be correction of the faulty thinking that has led to the guilt. In either case the guilt must be dealt with.

Another barrier to communication is *mishandled hostility*. All marriage partners occasionally do things that aggravate the other partner. When the annoyance is suppressed, it tends to build up and comes out in hostility such as snide remarks, avoidance of the other's needs, indifference, and other tactics. Repressed anger can lead to psychosomatic illnesses and depression (see chapter 9).

Still another barrier to communication is *manipulation*, or using the communication process to get one's own way rather than to solve the problem. For true communication to take place, partners need to recognize and overcome the barriers to communication as well as utilize the communication guidelines suggested earlier.

NEEDS MUST BE MET

Speaking of meeting one another's needs in marriage, the Clinebells write "Intimacy is not so much a matter of what or how much is shared as it is *the degree of mutual need-satisfaction within the relationship*" (Clinebell 1970, 1). They suggest four basic needs that must be met in marriage for the growth of intimacy (Clinebell 1970, 69-76). One need is *security*. This is the need for stability and safety. This need can be met by a partner's being faithful and responsible. It involves supporting one's partner in times of failure, grief, disappointment, and pain. It is providing a psychological and emotional haven for one's partner.

Another need is *self-esteem*. This involves a person's sense of self-worth, his or her value as a person. Couples often tear down each other's self-esteem without even being aware of it. A classic example is Archie Bunker calling Edith a "dingbat." Both partners need to reaffirm each other's self-worth continually. As the Clinebells say, *"Whatever else you neglect, don't neglect your mate's self-esteem"* (Clinebell 1970, 71).

A third need is *love*. Each of us needs to know that someone else cares for us deeply. Many psychologists believe this is the most basic of all needs. See Table 11-1 for the distinction between immature and mature love.

True love, or *agape* love, is more than an emotion or a romantic feeling. As we have already pointed out, it is an act of the will. As one chooses to love another, and acts on that choice, the feelings will follow. A counselee may tell a counselor, "I am not in love any more." What the counselee means is that there are no more warm, romantic feelings. Love is not something one falls into or out of, it is something one does. As the Bible puts it, *Above all, love each other deeply, because love covers over a multitude of sins* (1 Pet. 4:8).

The fourth need is *pleasure.* While this includes the need for sex, it goes beyond it. We all need to experience enjoyment. Marriage partners should provide pleasure for each other. One's marriage partner should be one's best friend. Sex in marriage should not be a duty or something tacked onto marriage. Sex should be an integral part of marriage. It should be an opportunity for partners to give and receive pleasure. It is a physical way for a couple to express their oneness.

GOD NEEDS TO BE INVOLVED

A marriage will never be all it could be apart from God. God must be involved not only in the life of each partner, but in the partnership as well. We can picture the relationship between a couple and God as a triangle (see Figure 11-1). As the partners draw closer to God they draw closer to each other. Bible study and prayer should be an important part of marriage. Counselors should encourage Christian couples to spend time together in prayer and Bible study on a regular basis if they are not already doing so.

FAMILY COUNSELING

Family counseling involves problems that reach beyond the married couple to other members of the family such as children and in-laws. A family is an integrated network and should be seen as a whole.

When dealing with families we can follow the seven steps of Reality Therapy with each member of the family. A lay counselor involved in counseling with families needs to have a basic understanding of the family as a social unit. The counselor should also know something about human development from infancy to adulthood and about parent-child relationships.

The six principles discussed under marriage counseling also apply to family counseling. First, all families have problems. Second, the family is a system and must be approached as such. Third, usually the most effective approach is to involve all family members. Fourth, communication is the key to family problems. Parents and children must really listen to each other. Fifth, children have needs too. Parents should be aware of these needs. For children, self-esteem is critical. Sixth, God needs to be involved. While it is impor-

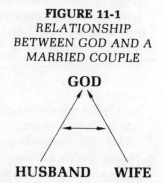

FIGURE 11-1
RELATIONSHIP BETWEEN GOD AND A MARRIED COUPLE

GOD

HUSBAND   WIFE

tant for a family to develop some type of family devotions, God should not just be tacked on at the end of the day. The Lord needs to be involved in all aspects of family life. He should be part of every decision and present at every activity. It is especially important for children to see that God is part of their everyday life and not relegated to a couple of hours on Sunday.

The home can be a place of joy, warmth, and happiness. It can also be the most miserable place on earth. More than half a million children run away, (Conger 1977, 571), and over a million husbands and wives leave each other every year (Lasswell 1982, 389). Many of these families can be helped and homes healed. Marriage and family counseling can be effective. The books listed at the end of the chapter can help a counselor begin developing a working knowledge of these areas. Because the family is a system, family counseling can become quite complex. Counseling with three or more persons is not just individual counseling multiplied by three or more. The complexity of the relationship is geometric (see Figure 11-2). Because of this geometric expansion of relationships, it requires great skill to engage in family counseling. For this reason, we suggest that lay counselors be alert to the seriousness of the problems a family faces and be prepared to make a professional referral (see chapter 13). Lay and professional counselors together can minister to families.

DISCUSSION QUESTIONS

1. How were decisions made in the family in which you grew up? How were resources (money, time, etc.) handled? What were the patterns of communication? What were the things you could not talk about? Were emotions expressed openly? Did your parents entertain frequently? How do (or might, if you are single) all these rules affect your marriage?
2. What types of problems have arisen in your marriage or family? How were they resolved? Would counseling have helped?
3. How important is premarital counseling? Why?
4. Diagram the relationships in your family following the example of Figure 11-2. Did you realize there were

so many? What are the implications of this complexity?

FIGURE 11-2

*COMPLEXITY OF INTERPERSONAL RELATION-
SHIPS AS FAMILY SIZE INCREASES*

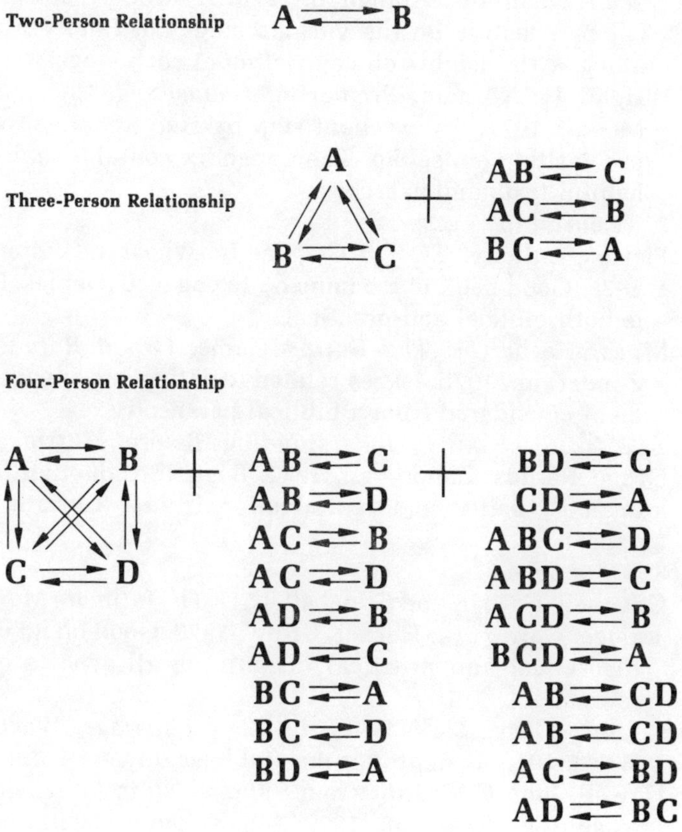

Two-Person Relationship   A ⇌ B

Three-Person Relationship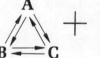

Four-Person Relationship

   +

A B ⇌ C	BD ⇌ C
A B ⇌ D	CD ⇌ A
A C ⇌ B	A B C ⇌ D
A C ⇌ D	A B D ⇌ C
A D ⇌ B	A C D ⇌ B
A D ⇌ C	B C D ⇌ A
B C ⇌ A	A B ⇌ CD
B C ⇌ D	A B ⇌ CD
B D ⇌ A	A C ⇌ BD
	A D ⇌ B C

SUGGESTED READING

1. *Marriage and Family Counseling*
Haley, Jay and Hoffman, Lynn. *Techniques of Family Therapy*. New York: Basic Books, 1967. A systems approach to family counseling.
Hulme, William E. *The Pastoral Care of Families*. Nashville: Abingdon, 1962 (Biblical approach).
Stewart, Charles W. *The Minister as Marriage Counselor*. Nashville: Abingdon, 1970. A strong theological perspective on the various stages of family life along with insights on counseling at each stage.
Wright, H. Norman. *Premarital Counseling*. Chicago: Moody, 1977. An excellent step-by-step treatment of premarital counseling. The appendix contains many helpful tests and exercises.
2. *Courtship*
Florio, Anthony. *Two to Get Ready*. Wheaton: Victor, 1978. Good book to recommend to engaged couples. It is both biblical and practical.
Miles, Herbert J. *The Dating Game*. Grand Rapids: Zondervan, 1975. Issues related to dating and engagement considered from a biblical perspective.
_____. *Sexual Understanding Before Marriage*. Grand Rapids: Zondervan, 1971. Basic introduction to human sexuality and reproduction from a Christian perspective.
3. *Marriage*
Clinebell, H. J., Jr. and Clinebell, C. H. *The Intimate Marriage*. New York: Harper & Row, 1970. Good blend of theoretical and practical insights on all aspects of intimacy.
Collins, Gary. *Make More of Your Marriage*. Waco: Word, 1976. Insights for marital harmony.
Howell, John C. *Equality and Submission in Marriage*. Nashville: Broadman, 1979. A balanced presentation

of the partnership versus hierarchy controversy in Christian marriage.

4. *Communications*

Leaman, David R. *Making Decisions.* Scottdale, Pa.: Herald, 1979. An aid to couples in decision making.

Scanzoni, John. *Love and Negotiate.* Waco: Word, 1979. View that conflict in marriage can be handled without being a destructive force.

Scoresby, A. Lynn. *The Marriage Dialogue.* Reading, Mass.: Addison-Wesley, 1977. Coverage of all areas of marriage communication.

Wright, H. Norman. *Communication: Key to Your Marriage.* Wheaton: Victor, 1978. A biblical perspective on communication in marriage. It contains useful exercises for couples.

_____. *The Family That Listens.* Wheaton: Victor, 1978. Presentation of the viewpoint that communication begins with listening and listening requires skills.

5. *Family*

Hendricks, Howard. *Heaven Help the Home.* Wheaton: Victor, 1973. A well-written book with practical suggestions for family living.

Martin, Dorothy. *Creative Family Worship.* Chicago: Moody, 1976. A good treatment of this essential aspect of family life.

Petersen, J. Allen. *For Families Only.* Wheaton: Tyndale, 1977. A collection of articles dealing with various aspects of family life from a Christian perspective.

6. *Children*

Dobson, James. *Dare to Discipline.* Wheaton: Tyndale, 1970. A treatment of discipline from a practical Christian perspective.

_____. *Hide or Seek.* Old Tappan, N.J.: Revell, 1974. A consideration of the important topic of self-esteem.

Meier, Paul. *Christian Child-rearing and Personality Development.* Grand Rapids: Baker, 1977. Coverage of human development through adolescence, with applications.

7. *Sex*

Grant, Wilson. *From Parent to Child about Sex.* Grand Rapids: Zondervan, 1973. Sex education in the home.

Johnson, Rex. *At Home with Sex.* Wheaton: Victor, 1979. Helps for parents dealing with sex in the home.

Wheat, E. and Wheat, G. *Intended for Pleasure.* Old Tappan, N.J.: Revell, 1977. A Christian sex manual.

CHAPTER TWELVE

Drug Dependency

I woo with every charm the tempter knows
I promise comfort with a secret leer
I soothe with liquid fire that smoulders with desire
And leaves the ash of caution as it glows.

I lead you down a path so smooth and gay.
The spectre at the end you do not see
Until you find you must depend on me
To fight the growing panic on the way.

And at the end, I leave you to your fate
To learn what I have done to you, too late (Bassett).

So the seductive charm of mood-altering drugs has been sought, and so the seekers have been seduced and reduced in an ongoing process as old as recorded history. Ruth Bassett's poem, above, describes that process well, from promised charm to panic to one's eventual undoing. In modern times, the various drug alternatives have multiplied, but the effects remain the same, in all too many instances.

Mr. Thomas Schultz is a respected, successful business man in his community. About a year ago he began having a severe cash flow problem in his business caused by inflation and a slowdown in orders. He began to experience pain in his upper back and neck and he had increased difficulty falling asleep and staying asleep. After several weeks, he went to see his physician. When he presented himself, haggard and weary, and told his story, the doctor prescribed a minor tranquilizer to reduce the muscle spasms in Tom's back and to allow him to get much-needed sleep. With the medication he was able to relax somewhat and began to sleep more easily; gradually, however, the former condition reappeared and Tom began taking more of the medication. He found that he required more medication to achieve the same results, and he needed his sleep badly. Then his physician expressed concern at the number of refills of the prescription and announced that they would need to reduce and discontinue the medication. Tom began to panic.

Mitch is a 15-year-old high school student, a typical youngster from an average, middle-class family. He has attended Sunday school and church regularly and has gotten along with his parents. Some friends at school introduced him to marijuana. At first "smoking dope" was a scary, daring thing to do and he did it to feel like a part of his group. However, lately he has noticed that no matter what his friends are doing or what his parents or anyone else is thinking, he has a deep desire to re-experience the euphoria of pot. The next opportunity to get high has become a preoccupation. His school work has begun to falter, he has little time for some of his old friends, and his parents have noticed that he has become irritable and noncommunicative. Last week his father found some paraphernalia in his room, a pipe, some cigarette papers, and a plastic bag of marijuana. An angry confrontation led to Mitch being grounded. Today he is pacing his room, feeling panicky and angry.

Mrs. Clara Johnson is a homemaker. For seventeen years she faithfully carried out the tasks that everyone expected of her; she was variously housekeeper, seamstress, chauffeur, lover, short-order cook, Sunday school teacher, part-time employee, mother confessor, family calendar keeper, nurse, companion, disciplinarian, hostess. This past fall, with the oldest of her five children at age 15 and the youngest 9, she found herself dreading three o'clock and the sequence of children trooping in with their various requests and demands. A friend suggested that a glass of wine at about 2:30 P.M. ("for your stomach's sake," she said) would calm her nerves and prepare her for the most demanding hours of her day. It worked. Each day at about half past two she poured herself a half glass of wine—gradually it grew to more than half—and she could feel herself relax. Midwinter vacation came, the children's schedule was changed, but she still maintained her ritual. Then, on the last day of vacation, her daughter, Sheila, walked into the kitchen just as mother was having her relaxant. Surprised and slightly upset, she challenged her mother's drinking and asked her not to do it. Clara agreed. The days that followed were worse than ever. By three o'clock each day Clara found herself becoming tense, irritable, and unreasonable. She began to consider how she could resume her wine-for-relaxation ritual without Sheila—or anyone else—knowing.

All three of these persons, Tom, Mitch, and Clara, have a problem. They are drug dependent; their use of chemicals began in understandable ways. Their dependency was a function of their needs and the ability of the chemical to meet their needs.

DEFINITIONS

In order to understand the issues involved in this critical area of human need (drug dependence is now America's number three health problem) (Goodell et al. 1978, 3), we need to learn some definitions. First of all, what is a drug? A drug should be defined as any substance, without nutritional value, that when taken into the living organism may modify one or more of its functions (Taber's 1975, 61-62).

What do we mean by drug dependence? According to *Taber's Cyclopedic Medical Dictionary* drug dependence is

A psychic (and sometimes physical) state resulting from interaction of a living organism and a drug. Characterized by behavorial and other responses that include a compulsion to take the drug on a continuous or periodic basis in order to experience its psychic effects or to avoid the discomfort of its absence. Tolerance may or may not be present and a person may be dependent on more than one drug (Taber's 1975, 65).

Drug dependence, then, refers to a broad category of interactions including many substances that are very common in our society In addition to those things that we commonly call drugs we need to include caffeine, nicotine, and alcohol. As a matter of fact, these are the most used and abused drugs in the United States today. In the opinion of virtually all authorities, alcohol is by far the most abused drug and alcoholism is the most prevalent drug dependence. In the mid-sixties the national incidence rate was 4.5 per 100 for a total of approximately 5 million alcoholics (McCarthy 1964, 195); by the late 1970s the incidence rate had increased and it was estimated that there were 10 million alcoholics in the U.S. Only 3 percent of these are "Skid Row" types; the remainder are part of the general population of our country (Goodell 1978, 3).

Since alcoholism is the most prevalent drug dependency, and since most treatment programs do not differentiate between alcoholism and other dependencies such as amphetamines, barbiturates, and hallucinogens, the major portion of this chapter will focus on alcohol use, abuse, and dependency.

Alcoholism has been defined in various ways. We suggest that alcoholism is best understood as a primary illness which is progressive, incurable, and fatal if not treated (Blum 1974, 37-47). Alcoholism meets the accepted criteria of medical science as an illness or a disease.* It is characterized by a definite set of symptoms, follows a process that is predictable, and results in both physical and behavioral pathology.

Expressing concern over physicians' "poor track record" in dealing with the alcoholic patient, Dr. Joe Norquist and his associates characterize alcoholism clearly and succinctly:

> *Alcoholism has been recognized as a disease by the American Medical Association since 1957. The American Psychiatric Association, The American College of Physicians, The World Health Organization, The Department of Justice, and many insurance companies also label alcoholism as a disease, that is "a definite*

---

*In dealing with alcoholism as an illness or disease we are not excusing the alcoholic nor are we absolving the alcoholic of responsibility for his or her condition. Rather, by viewing alcoholism as an illness or disease, we may attack the problem rather than the person. "Both medical doctors and insurance companies accept alcoholism as a disease because it is predictable, progressive, and treatable. The disease concept of alcoholism helps both the alcoholic and his or her family to seek treatment." (John Kolenberg with Kay Oliver Lewis, "Helping the Alcoholic in Your Church," *Moody Monthly*, November 1981, p. 15.)

morbid process having a characteristic train of symptoms, affecting the whole body or any of its parts; having an etiology, pathology and prognosis which may be known or unknown."

Though the particular disease of alcoholism is presently not curable, it is treatable and controllable. Much like diabetes mellitus, where sugar is poison for the diabetic, alcohol is poison for the alcoholic. Where the diabetic must avoid sugar, the alcoholic must avoid alcohol.

Early detection and prevention of alcoholism are clearly essential and require both an informed public and a knowledgeable medical profession. Alcohol use is an accepted part of our culture and most Americans have only a limited awareness of the dangerous and psychoactive effects of this drug. This side of alcohol has been minimized and its victims often ignored. It must be made abundantly clear: ALCOHOL IS AN ADDICTIVE DRUG (Goodell 1978, 5).

We now turn to a consideration of diagnosis and intervention for alcoholics and other drug dependent persons.

DIAGNOSIS AND INTERVENTION

Until recently it has been thought that it is necessary for the alcoholic to "hit bottom" in order to recover. The result was that alcoholism was not acknowledged until the person was in the chronic, late stage with severe medical problems. By then he had lost all social status. Dr. Richard Heilman, Director of the Alcohol and Drug Unit at the Veterans Administration Hospital in Minneapolis, writes, "It is most unfortunate that we wait until complications develop before we define or diagnose the alcoholic. No other illness is defined or diagnosed on the basis of the complications it causes" (Heilman). Dr. Heilman, himself a recovering alcoholic as well as a distinguished physician and psychiatrist, goes on to suggest a list of eight signs of alcohol dependence (he notes that with the exception of item 6, these apply to other drugs as well):

1. *Preoccupation* with alcohol or the next opportunity to drink.
2. *Increased tolerance* for alcohol. Can usually drink much more than others and still function relatively well.
3. *Gulping drinks.* Usually drinks a "double" or the first couple of drinks fairly fast.
4. *Drinks alone.* This includes drinking in public in bars, but by oneself.
5. *Use as a "medicine"* for relief of tension or anxiety or as an aid to sleep.
6. *Blackout.* Drinking quantities sufficient to cause morning after "amnesia" for some of the events of the previous evening.
7. *Secluded bottle.* Having a bottle secluded in the home or elsewhere in case a drink is "needed."
8. *Non-premeditated drinking.* Drinking much more than planned, or drinking differently than one had previously planned.

Questions that will help a counselor understand which of these indications are positive are contained in Table 12-1. Which areas are positive will indicate whether or not a person is drug dependent as well as the type of dependency represented.

TYPES OF ALCOHOL DEPENDENCE

Following the clues provided by Dr. E. M. Jellinek (Jellinek 1968), the Yale University physiologist of a generation ago, many authorities find it helpful to think in terms of differing types of alcohol addiction.

TABLE 12-1

QUESTIONS FOR DETECTING THE EIGHT SIGNS OF ALCOHOL DEPENDENCE

The following questions are suggested for each of the eight criteria. If four or more of the eight criteria are fulfilled with a "yes" or "sometimes" answer, this constitutes an alcoholic or drug dependent or non-social drinking pattern and constitutes positive evidence of alcoholism. (Note: Same questions can be used whatever the drug of choice, except for blackout questions.)

1. Preoccupation

Do you find yourself looking forward to the end of a day's work so you can have a couple of drinks and relax?

Do you look forward to the end of the week so you can have some fun drinking?

Does the thought of drinking sometimes enter your mind when you should be thinking of something else?

Do you sometimes feel the need to have a drink at a particular time of the day?

2. Increased Tolerance

Do you find that you can sometimes drink more than others and not show it too much?

Have friends ever commented on your ability to "hold your liquor"?

Have you ever wondered about your increased capacity to drink and may be somewhat proud of this ability?

Do you usually have an extra drink when mixing drinks for others?

3. Gulping Drinks

Do you usually order a double or like to drink your first two or *three drinks fairly fast?*

Do you usually have a couple of drinks before going to a party or out to dinner?

4. Drinking Alone

Do you sometimes stop in a bar and have a couple of drinks by yourself?

Do you sometimes drink at home alone or when no one else is drinking?

Do you usually have an extra drink by yourself when mixing drinks for others?

5. Use as a Medicine

Do you usually drink to calm your nerves or reduce tension?

Do you find it difficult to enjoy a party or dance if there is nothing to drink?

Do you commonly use alcohol as a nightcap to help you get to sleep at night?

Do you commonly use alcohol to relieve physical discomfort?

6. Blackout

In the morning following an evening of drinking, have you ever had the experience of not being able to remember everything that happened on the night before?

Have you ever had difficulty recalling how you got home after a night's drinking?

7. Secluded Bottle

Do you sometimes store a bottle away around the house in the event you may "need" a drink?

Do you ever keep a bottle in the trunk of your car or office desk "just in case" you might need a drink?

8. Nonpremeditated Drinking

Do you sometimes stop in to have a drink or two and have several more than you had planned?

Do you sometimes find yourself stopping in for a drink when you had planned to go straight home or someplace else?

Do you sometimes drink more than you think you should?

Is your drinking sometimes different from what you would like it to be?

Alpha type • This pattern of usage suggests psychological dependence. The person uses alcohol to relieve tension (like Clara Johnson at the beginning of the chapter) or to lose physical pain and has come to depend on it for the symptomatic relief. This type does not involve "loss of control" or the inability to abstain. Approximately 10-15 percent of those in Alcoholics Anonymous (A.A.) represent this type.

Beta type • Persons in this group have begun experiencing medical complications relatively early in their drinking experience and thus have not progressed to the characteristics of the gamma type; instead, they show signs of bodily illness such as pancreatitis, severe gastritis, or liver disease. Usually they continue drinking even after they are advised that their pain is directly related to their use of alcohol. They are drug dependent!

Gamma type • This group, which makes up the majority of the persons in A.A., shows the characteristics normally associated with alcoholism. The most obvious sign is loss of control. Pathologically, after the person has one or two drinks, he seems unable to exert normal control and continues to drink even though it may cost him everything of value. One of the authors has noted this pathology with successful people of unusual personal character. Their achievements evidence strong will—yet after they ingest alcohol their will seems nonexistent.

Other signs include increased tolerance and with-drawal symptoms. "Increased tolerance" refers to adaptive changes in the person's cells and tissue which allow, in fact require, that more of the drug be used (tolerated) in order to achieve a specific level of sedation (intoxication). "Withdrawal symptoms" is a term referring to a wide range of psychological and physical discomfort experienced when the gamma type dependent reduces his intake of alcohol or attempts to abstain after a period of drinking. (It is sometimes called "the abstinence syndrome.") These include anxiety, trembling ("the shakes"), nausea, vomiting; they may extend to convulsions and auditory and visual hallucinations; in delirium tremens, they may cause death. In fact, 15 percent of those cases that experience the neurological symptoms of delirium end in death (Thorn 1977, 712).

Delta type • This group experiences all of the signs of the gamma type except that "loss of control" is not characteristic; instead, one sees the "inability to abstain." This person is apparently able to control his or her drinking at tolerable levels. This type of alcoholism is seen in France where many men and women continue for many years; finally they develop severe medical symptoms without ever losing control.

OTHER DRUGS: "UPPERS," "DOWNERS," AND HALLUCINOGENS

For the purposes of this manual, all other drugs can be classified as "uppers" or stimulants, "downers" (central nervous system depressants, tranquilizers and sedatives), and hallucinogens (drugs with high potential for producing euphoric and hallucinatory experiences). See Table 12-2 for a description of various drugs.

Stimulants • These include popular everyday drugs like caffeine and nicotine as well as prescribed medications

TABLE 12-2

CLASSIFICATION OF DRUGS

Name	Chemical Name	Classification	Duration of Effects	Long-term Symptoms	Physically Addictive
Heroin Horse Smack Junk H	Diacetyl-morphine	Narcotic	4 hours	Addiction Constipation Loss of appetite	Yes
Mescaline	Mescaline	Hallucinogen	Varies	Panic reaction Psychosis	Minimally
Cocaine Coke Snow Star Dust	Methylester of Benzoylec-gonine	Stimulant Anesthesia	Brief	Depression Convulsions Nose bleeds	Yes
PCP Angel Dust Super Weed Busy Bee	Phencyclidine	Veterinary anesthetic Hallucinogen	Varies	Hallucinations Seizures Coma	Not yet determined

Name	Chemical Name	Classification	Duration of Effects	Long-term Symptoms	Physically Addictive
LSD Acid Sugar	D-lysergic acid	Hallucinogen	10 hours	Panic reaction Psychosis	Usually not
Methedrine Speed	Methedrine	Sympathomimetic	4 hours	Delusions Toxic Psychosis	Yes
Benzedrine Bennies Uppers	Benzedrine	Sympathomimetic	4 hours	Delusions Toxic Psychosis	Yes
Phennies Yellow Jacket Peanuts	Phenobarbital	Sedative-hypnotic Barbiturate	4 hours	Severe with-drawal symptoms Convulsions	Yes
Marijuana Pot Grass Tea Reefer	Cannabis Sativa	Euphoriant Hallucinogen	2-4 hours	Mild impair-ment of motor reflexes	In some cases
Methadone Dolly	Dolophine Amidone	Narcotic	4-6 hours	Addiction Constipation	Yes

Name	Chemical Name	Classification	Duration of Effects	Long-term Symptoms	Physically Addictive
Alcohol Booze Juice	Ethanol Ethyl Alcohol	Sedative-hypnotic	1-4 hours	Cirrhosis Toxic psychosis Neurological damage	Yes
Tobacco Coffin Nail Stick	Nicotiana Tabacum	Stimulant-sedative	Varies	Emphysema Lung Cancer Cardiovascular damage	Yes
Caffeine Coffee Tea Many soft drinks Chocolate	Caffeine	Stimulant	Varies	Insomnia Anxiety Depression	Yes

such as dexedrine, benzedrine, and others of a class generally referred to as amphetamines. The most common of these stimulants, coffee, does have potential for dependency of the alpha class. In extreme cases, where coffee drinking is very heavy over a long period, people have been known to develop the dependence characteristics of tolerance change and withdrawal symptoms; however, since loss of control is not an issue and since the most severe result is change of mood, the dependency potential of caffeine is generally ignored. As with nicotine its more serious health problems are related to effect on body organs; so heavy coffee drinkers may develop gastrointestinal discomfort while heavy smokers have increased potential for heart disease, respiratory diseases, and cancer.

More significant drug dependence concerns stimulant drugs that produce hyperactivity. With prolonged use these have a potential for brain damage and even for a lethal overdose. This is true of the amphetamines. These drugs, designed for use in weight loss, in the treating of narcolepsy (sleeping sickness) and sometimes for treating certain cases of hyperactivity in children, are very dangerous when taken without regular medical supervision. The signs of use are high energy, easy excitability, flights of thought, euphoria, irritability, restlessness, and, after long usage, paranoid thoughts and disconnected thinking. Presently the stimulants have limited medical usage; in fact, their helpfulness for weight loss is considered negligible by most physicians. Consequently the predominant usage today is to create instant energy. Stimulants are so used, and abused, by persons who have less energy than they need or think they need. Such usage is at best questionable and is very dangerous.

Depressants • These include alcohol, a central nervous system (CNS) depressant, and other CNS depressants such as the minor tranquilizers (valium, librium, etc.), the opiates (including morphine, heroin, codeine, etc.), and the barbiturates (including phenobarbital and pentobarbital). These drugs, sometimes thought of as "sleepers" or "downers," reduce tension and anxiety, relax muscles, and decrease nerve sensitivity (thus producing relief from pain). These drugs have many legitimate medical uses; however, they all have a high risk for abuse and for gamma type addiction with potential for death. Depressants as a class are very dangerous when used in combination with alcoholic beverages since the combined effect can shut down neurological pathways and lead to heart arrest and/or cessation of breathing.

The signs of their abuse include constricted and/or "sleepy" eye stare (sometimes described as "vacant"), slowed speech and movement, increased sleep and dozing, and moderate to severe personality changes from slightly reduced inhibition to an apparent loss of caring and value orientation. Depressants play a large role in serious accidents, suicides, and homicides.

Hallucinogens • These drugs are capable of producing hallucinations or distortions of reality in one or more of the sensory systems. That is, the person taking the drugs sees, hears, smells, tastes, or feels things that do not exist or he greatly distorts things that do exist. Sometimes input to one sensory system produces sensations in another sensory system. For example, music may produce sensations of color or a color may produce a sensation of taste. One of the best known hallucinogens is D-lysergic acid (LSD). Another widely used hallucinogen is mescaline. Mescaline is milder and less dangerous than LSD. Both LSD and mescaline are generally taken orally. The most dangerous of all the hallucinogens is phencyclidine (PCP). On the street, PCP is commonly called "Angel Dust." The use of PCP is spreading rapidly. PCP can be injected, taken orally, sniffed, and smoked.

Reactions to PCP are generally unpredictable. PCP often leads to psychotic reactions with symptoms similar to paranoid schizophrenia. Acute toxic reactions from PCP can last up to a week and flashbacks can occur months later.

Some authorities would include cocaine and paint or glue sniffing under hallucinogens. Others would include marijuana. Regardless of where these drugs are included, they are dangerous and can lead to dependency.

INTERVENTION AND TREATMENT OF DRUG DEPENDENCY

Dr. Vernon E. Johnson, founder of the Johnson Institute programs in several states, a rehabilitation program for alcoholism, has developed an approach to intervention that is compatible with a counseling emphasis on relationship, responsibility, and religion. He says,

The primary factor within this...condition...is the delusion, or impaired judgment, which keeps the harmfully dependent person locked into his self-destructive pattern. It must be met and dealt with first (and on a continuing basis), since it blocks his entering any therapeutic process at all. The [dependent person] evades or denies outright any need for help whenever he is approached. It must be remembered that he is not in touch with reality. But even at his sickest, he is capable of accepting some useful portion of reality, if that reality is presented to him in forms he can receive (Johnson 1973, 44).

Johnson goes on to suggest some basic rules for presenting reality to the drug dependent person:

1. Meaningful persons must present the facts or data. . . .

2. The data presented should be specific and de-

scriptive of events *which have happened* or conditions *which exist.* . . .

3. The tone of the confrontation should not be judgmental. . . .

4. The chief evidence should be tied directly into [the
drug use] whenever possible. . . .

5. The evidence of behavior should be presented in
some detail, to give the [dependent] person a
panoramic view of himself during a given period
of time. . . .

6. The goal of the intervention, through the presentation of this material, is to have him see and accept
enough reality so that, however grudgingly, he can
accept in turn his need for help.

7. At this point, the available choices acceptable to
the interveners may be offered (Johnson 1973, 44).

The ministry of lay counselors focuses on the intervention process and on referring the dependent person for
treatment. We are not in a position to treat drug dependent persons. But organizations such as Alcoholics
Anonymous, Alcoholics Victorious, Alanon, Alateen,
and other private, religious, or state alcoholism or drug
addiction programs are equipped to deal with these persons. We need to be conscious of our competence boundaries.

PREVENTION

An area in which lay persons can have an effective
ministry is in prevention of drug dependency. Drug
dependency is the result of a process. If we can short-
circuit the process, we may be able to prevent dependency. A number of things can be done. First, we need to
strengthen the family. The family can provide the support a person needs. The family can provide the right
moral climate. The family can be a source of strength.

Many drug dependency problems are related to family problems. In research conducted among thousands of high school and college students, Charlie Shedd found that the one thing that most non-users had in common was "a feeling of closeness in the family circle" (Shedd 1971, 29).

Second, we can *meet psychological needs.* Drug dependency often results from unmet psychological needs. If a person can have these needs met in positive and healthy ways, there would be no need to turn to drugs. This is an area where the local church can be involved. The body of believers can provide support and encouragement.

Third, *eliminate spiritual vacuums.* Drugs are sometimes used to fill a void. Persons who are in a right relationship with God have a source of strength and a sense of purpose. God can meet people's deepest needs, but they need to allow Him to do so. As Christian lay counselors we can help people see how God can meet their needs.

Fourth, we can *provide accurate information.* We need to educate people as to the nature of drug dependency and the effects of various drugs. Drug education needs to be factual and rational, not hysterical and emotional. The local church can transmit this information through the Sunday school, youth groups, and general community education.

Finally, we can work to *reduce the availability of drugs.* We can work for legislation that would prevent pharmacies from renewing prescriptions for amphetamines or barbiturates. We can advocate stronger drug enforcement in our communities and schools. We also need to reduce the availability of alcohol, especially to teenagers. With the preventive steps discussed above, we can help individuals to avoid a dependency on drugs.

DISCUSSION QUESTIONS

1. Is one type of drug dependence more harmful than another? Which type is most serious?
2. Were you surprised to find caffeine listed as a drug? Why?
3. What is your reaction to the idea of alcoholism as a disease? Why?
4. All of the eight signs of alcohol dependence, except the sixth (see Table 12-1), apply to other drugs. Do you ever see any of these signs in yourself or others you know in relation to caffeine or prescription drugs?
5. Why is it important to confront the drug dependent person with reality and the facts?
6. Have you ever known a drug dependent person in your local church? How did the body minister to that one? How did you react?

SUGGESTED READING

Barnette, Henlee. The Drug Crisis and the Church. Philadelphia: Westminster, 1971. The role and ministry of the church.

Bergel, F. and Davies, D. All about Drugs. New York: Barnes & Noble, 1970. A basic introduction to the various drugs, their classification, use, effects, and other pertinent information.

Clinebell, Howard J. Understanding and Counseling the Alcoholic. Nashville: Abingdon, 1956. Geared for pastors, but with much useful information for the lay person.

Johnson, Vernon E. I'll Quit Tomorrow. New York: Harper & Row, 1973. An excellent book by a minister and authority on alcoholism. The book deals with the signs, symptoms, causes, and treatment of alcoholism. Many of the points made in this book are applicable to other forms of drug dependency.

Shedd, Charlie W. *Is Your Family Turned On?* Waco:
Word, 1971. A well researched book by a popular
writer. Shedd argues that the best safeguards against
drugs are a warm, loving, accepting family and spiritual values.

Shipp, T. J. *Helping the Alcoholic and His Family.* Philadelphia: Fortress, 1963. The effects of drug dependency on the dependent person and the whole family.
We must be prepared to minister to all of them.

Wegscheider, Sharon. *Another Chance.* Palo Alto, Calif.:
Science & Behavior, 1981. An excellent approach to the
problem of alcoholism and drug abuse from a family
systems perspective.

CHAPTER THIRTEEN

Referrals

When asked to define the difference between a neurotic and a psychotic, a college professor said, "Neurotics build castles in the air; psychotics live in them; and psychiatrists collect the rent." We may laugh at the professor's response, but the fact that many people have distorted impressions of reality or are out of touch with reality is a serious matter. As we counsel with people we may deal with some whose problems are more serious than we can handle. In that case, we need to refer these people to someone who is competent and available to help them. Gary Collins has said, "One of the most significant ways in which we can help people is to refer them and sometimes take them to more professional sources of help" (Collins 1976, 108). In this chapter, we want to discuss when, where, and how to refer people.

WHEN TO REFER

William B. Oglesby, a professor of pastoral counseling, suggests that the reasons for making referrals generally fall into one of three categories. They are competence, time, and emotional barriers (Oglesby 1969, 36-37).

COMPETENCE

While it may seem obvious, we need to be reminded that the most important reason for referring a person elsewhere is to provide help. If we are counseling someone who has a problem that we are not competent to handle, we need to refer him or her to someone who is competent. As pointed out in chapter 3, it is important for lay counselors to know their competence boundaries. Referring someone we are not competent to help is not a sign of inadequacy, weakness, or failure; rather it is a sign of genuine concern.

Persons who have serious mental or personality disorders usually need professional help. The problem most lay counselors face is determining when a problem is beyond their competence. Basically when a person's perception of reality is distorted or he is sufficiently depressed that normal functioning is affected or when a person is completely out of touch with reality, he should be referred to a professional. Whenever suicidal tendencies are present, a person should be referred to a professional. Table 13-1 contains a list of the signs and symptoms of abnormal behavior. All of us exhibit one or another of these symptoms at some time, but when these signs and symptoms are prolonged or severe or when a number of them appear together more serious psychological problems are indicated. In general, when a lay counselor is in doubt about his or her competence to minister effectively, the counselor should consult with his or her pastor or other qualified person.* We need to avoid the temptation to be exclusive or "Lone Rangers." We need to work with the leaders of the church. The pastor and the elders

---

*It is usually appropriate to tell the counselee that one is going to request advice on the counselee's case, assuring the counselee that he or she will remain anonymous.

TABLE 13-1

SIGNS AND SYMPTOMS OF ABNORMAL BEHAVIOR (Collins 1972, 53-67)

1. Faulty Perception
a. *Reduced Sensitivity—sight, hearing, touch, etc.*
b. *Increased Sensitivity*
c. *Distorted Sensitivity—illusions, stimuli present but not interpreted correctly*
d. *Hallucinations—perception with no stimuli present*

2. Distorted Thinking
a. *Obsessions—persistent recurrence of some unpleasant impulse or thought*
b. *Phobias—irrational fears*
c. *Delusions—false beliefs*
  (1) Persecution
  (2) Delusions of grandeur

3. Faulty Emotional Expression
a. *Flat Affect—showing no emotion or unchanged expression*
b. *Elation or Euphoria—exaggerated feeling of well being*
c. *Depression—see chapter 9*
d. *Emotional Variability—wide mood swings over short periods*
e. *Inappropriate Affect—wrong emotional response to situation (i.e., smiling or laughing in a serious context)*
f. *Fear and Anxiety—overwhelming and incapacitating*

4. Unusual Motor Activity
a. *Overactivity—from what is normal for that person*
b. *Underactivity—from what is normal for that person*
c. *Compulsive Activity—repeating an act over and over*

5. Disorientation—*not being able to orient oneself in persons, place, and time*

6. Antisocial Behavior
a. *Overly Aggressive*
b. *Violent*
c. *Inappropriate Responses*
d. *Withdrawn*
e. *Inattentive*

should become part of the process.

TIME

There may be individuals who have problems that require a time commitment greater than we are able to make. Even if we are competent to handle a problem, we may not have the time to do so. In cases where a person's problem will require more time than we can give to it, it is proper to refer the person to someone who can devote the necessary time to his or her problem.

Also, when we become involved in a counseling ministry, particularly if it is effective, we may find that our caseload is growing too large. Here again it is appropriate to refer people. We each have only 24 hours a day and our energy and stress levels are limited. To take on too much is to place ourselves in jeopardy.

It is important for lay counselors not to develop what is often called a "Messiah Complex." We cannot help everyone. We may not be able to help some people because their problems are beyond our competence boundaries. We may not be able to help others because we do not have the time. We have our families and our own routine responsibilities. Allowing a counseling ministry to interfere with those areas will make a lay counselor ineffective. The counselor may soon become a counselee.

EMOTIONAL BARRIERS

There are times when we have both the time and the competence to counsel with someone and yet it may be best to refer them elsewhere. This is especially true if there are emotional barriers to effective counseling.

Counseling can be a very intense and intimate process. If we find we are emotionally involved with a counselee, it may be better to refer the person to someone else. This may be the case particularly in counseling with a person of the opposite sex. It goes without saying that the greatest caution and the utmost propriety are called for. Even with the greatest propriety and the best intentions it is possible for a counselor to become emotionally involved with a counselee of the opposite sex. When a counselor becomes aware that this is happening, it is often best to refer the counselee to someone else.* This should be done both in the counselee's best interest and for the counselor's own good.

We may find ourselves counseling with someone we personally dislike or toward whom we have negative feelings. If we are unable to change those feelings, we will be unable to give the counselee the best help. We need to be genuinely open; while we need to resolve our negative feelings, the counselee needs help, and he or she should not have to wait until we resolve our problem. We should refer that person to someone who can give help now.

We need to be careful about counseling with persons where there may be a conflict of interests. For example, it may not be effective to counsel with an employer or employee because the employer-employee relationship may enter the counseling process, and either party may respond out of his role identity rather than as he really feels. Self-awareness is important—in fact, it may be critical for the counselee's well being that the lay counselor be aware of and honest about his or her competence or time limitations or emotional conflicts.

---

*Some signs of becoming involved with a counselee of the opposite sex are prolonged sessions, flirtation by either party, and sexual arousal. Counseling is an intimate and private ministry, and it is easy for unhealthy emotional attachments to begin.

WHERE TO REFER

PASTOR

While there are a number of places to refer people, and we will suggest several, a logical place for the Christian lay counselor to begin is with his or her pastor. Most pastors have had some training in counseling during their preparation for the ministry. Many pastors with seminary training have spent at least one term in clinical pastoral education (CPE). Some pastors have had additional training in pastoral psychology and counseling.

In many cases, one's pastor will be able to handle those problems that are beyond the competence of the lay counselor. Even when the problem exceeds the pastor's competence, the pastor may still be a good source for finding someone who is competent. A pastor may have a colleague with specialized training or may know of a professional counselor with appropriate experience.

PROFESSIONAL COUNSELORS

There are four basic types of professional counselors or therapists. A *psychiatrist* is a medical doctor with an additional three-or four-year residency in psychiatry. A *clinical psychologist* generally holds a doctorate in clinical psychology and has had a one-year internship in psychotherapy. A *psychiatric social worker* holds a master of social work degree (MSW). This involves a two-year postgraduate course of study and internship in social work and psychotherapy. *Marriage and family therapists** can have a variety of education and training

---

*While the term *marriage and family counselor* is still used, *marriage and family therapist* is more widely accepted in professional circles today.

backgrounds. Although many of them are clinical psychologists, psychiatric social workers, or have other graduate degrees and training in counseling, some may have little or no training. While all states regulate and certify psychiatrists and psychologists, many states neither regulate nor certify marriage and family therapists. Where unlicensed professionals are concerned, it is important to ascertain if they are members of some professional certifying agency. In the case of marriage and family therapists, the most widely recognized agency is the American Association for Marriage and Family Therapy.

Before referring someone to a professional counselor one should consider his professional standing (is he licensed, is he a member of professional associations, etc.?), theoretical orientation (see chapter 4 for a discussion of the various schools of psychology), and reputation in the community. It is best for a lay counselor to have a personal acquaintance with the professional.

Christian lay counselors who deal with professional counselors are also concerned with religious beliefs. Should an evangelical lay counselor refer people only to evangelical professional counselors? There is no absolute answer to this question. In general, an evangelical lay counselor and counselee would do well to find a competent evangelical professional counselor. Counselees are more likely to be helped by someone with whom they are comfortable, and they are more likely to be comfortable with someone who shares their faith. An evangelical professional counselor will be able to utilize this shared faith as a resource, while a secular therapist may view one's faith as part of the problem rather than as a resource for helping. An evangelical counselor is better able to call on the resources of the church. Finally, an evangelical therapist would be in an appropriate position to deal with those aspects of the problem that concern spiritual issues.

While all of the above may be true, a competent evangelical therapist may not be available at a given time or in a certain place. A secular therapist may well be able to help an evangelical Christian. The major concern should be whether the therapist is sympathetic or antagonistic toward the faith of the counselee. A therapist who is sympathetic toward the faith of the counselee, even if the therapist does not share that faith, may be able to help the counselee.* Generally, one should attempt to find the most competent therapist available whose approach would not violate the faith of the counselee. A person who is severely depressed or mentally disturbed should not delay finding medical psychiatric care.

MEDICAL DOCTOR

As we have seen, some problems have a medical basis. If a lay counselor suspects that a problem has a medical basis, the counselee should be referred to a medical doctor. It is generally best to have a person see his own family physician. The family physician knows the person, has a case history, and may quickly spot changes from the person's normal physical state of being.

If a counselee does not have or does not want to use a family physician, the counselor should recommend a general practitioner or a family physician,** with whom the counselor is familiar and in whom he or she has confidence. It is generally not best to recommend a person to a specialist. The usual procedure is to have a person see a family physician who will refer the person to a specialist if it is necessary.

---

*It has been our experience that many non-evangelical psychiatrists are sympathetic to a sincere faith and view it as a resource. However, we recognize this is not always the case.

**A family physician is a medical doctor who has completed a three-year residency in family health care.

A word of warning should be sounded at this point. It is very important that lay counselors not try to play medical doctor. Counselors should not attempt to diagnose physical symptoms nor should they prescribe over-the-counter or home remedies. It is important to use the medical profession when dealing with physical problems and/or severe mental or emotional disorders. Where symptoms persist, it is always safe to have a physician evaluate the person to rule out any biological malfunctions.

OTHER PERSONS AND AGENCIES

There are many persons and agencies to which it may be appropriate to refer a counselee. A person with a legal problem should be referred to a lawyer or to the local legal aid society. In the case of child abuse or neglect the person should be referred to the state department of children and family services or local welfare departments. A person with a financial problem might be referred to a financial counselor or counseling service, the United Fund, or a state or county welfare agency. Many communities have family service agencies. None of us is an expert in everything. When we are counseling with those who have problems that are outside our competency boundaries, we need to refer them to an appropriate person or agency.

If we become involved in the ministry of counseling to any extent, we should begin to develop a file of professionals and agencies to which counselees may be referred. It is good to have names, addresses, and phone numbers readily available. It is more effective, when counseling, to have a place, at hand, to refer a counselee rather than trying to find one after the problem arises. In this area the pastor and church staff can be of real assistance.

HOW TO REFER

There are three basic aspects to referral: (1) making the decision to refer and where, (2) making contact, and (3) follow-up. Let us look at each of these aspects of the referral process.

THE DECISION TO REFER

Both the decision to refer and to whom to refer should be made jointly by the counselor and counselee. As the counselor becomes involved in counseling with an individual, the counselor may discover the counselee's problem is outside his or her areas of competence. At that point, the counselor should point out to the counselee that the problem appears to be beyond the counselor's expertise. He should then suggest that they consider finding someone with the training and experience to help. Prayer should play a part in the decision process. While it is appropriate for the counselor to suggest sources for referral, the counselee should make the final decision.

The only time a counselor should consider making a referral without the counselee's agreement is if the counselee is potentially self-destructive or violent. That is, if the counselee is going to hurt himself or herself or other people. At this point one should secure the cooperation of the counselee's family. In extreme cases a person may need to be committed against his or her will. However, as a general rule referrals should be discussed with the counselee who should make the final decision.

CONTACTING A PROFESSIONAL COUN- SELOR OR AGENCY

Generally it is best for counselees to make the appointment with a professional counselor or agency themselves. The counselor can supply the phone number and address but counselees should make their own arrangements. This insures that they are part of the decision process and it helps them to accept responsibility, an important part of the counseling process.

It is also common courtesy for the counselor to notify the person or agency that he or she is making a referral. That way, if additional information or assistance is needed, the counselor may be contacted. A counselor should only supply information to the referral source if it is requested and the counselee consents. A counselor should not divulge any information from counseling sessions without the counselee's permission. The only exception would be if a life is in danger, such as with a suicidal or violent counselee. Other than these most extreme cases, a counselor should never release information from counseling sessions.

Some professionals and agencies basically ignore lay counselors because they have no official standing. Others, however, will respond on a professional level. We should not be offended or feel hurt if a professional or agency does not respond to us personally. The issue is not our pride but the welfare of our counselees.

FOLLOW-UP

When a referral is made, we should generally step out of the picture and allow the professional to take over. It is important that we do nothing to undercut or interfere with the professional. We may still show interest in the counselee, ask about his well being, and give the counselee support. But we should not counsel the counselee about either the problem or the professional's treatment.

Sometimes after we make a referral a counselee may come to us and say that the professional is not helping and claim that we did a better job. At this point most lay counselors may be tempted to either take over the case themselves or make another referral. Generally, this temptation should be resisted. If the professional or agency has been properly checked out and if the decision to refer was mutually agreed upon by the counselor and counselee, then it is usually best to encourage the counselee to continue with the referral and discuss the matter directly with the professional. As Professor Eugene Kennedy says, "The general principle involved demands that once a referral is made we stay out of the picture and that we resist any impulse to assist or otherwise interfere with the newly developed relationship" (Kennedy 1977, 119).

Counseling is a difficult and challenging ministry. It is also a rewarding ministry. Christians who properly prepare themselves and develop the characteristics of effective counselors are able to have healing relationships. Each of us should take seriously the counseling opportunities that come our way, to prepare ourselves through study and prayer, and to minister to our brothers and sisters.

DISCUSSION QUESTIONS

1. *What are your competence boundaries in the area of counseling? How did you determine them?*
2. *Why is it sometimes difficult for counselors to accept the fact they cannot help some people? How can this be overcome?*
3. *Should lay counselors counsel with members of the opposite sex? Why? Under what circumstances?*
4. *Are you aware of qualified professionals and agencies in your community to whom you could refer people? How could you find them?*
5. *Why should a lay counselor avoid playing physician, lawyer, or therapist?*

SUGGESTED READING

Binder, V., Binder, A., and Rimland, B., eds. *Modern Therapies*. Englewood Cliffs, N.J.: Prentice-Hall, 1976. A collection of essays describing various types of therapies available from professional therapists.

Collins, Gary. *Fractured Personalities*. Carol Stream, Ill.: Creation House, 1972. A discussion of mental disorders, their causes, signs and symptoms, and treatment. A good introduction to abnormal psychology for the lay person.

Oates, Wayne and Neely, K. H. *Where To Go for Help*. Philadelphia: Westminster, 1972. A description of the various helping professions. It also contains a discussion on how to select a counselor. The largest part of this work deals with where to go for help with specific problems.

Oglesby, William B., Jr. *Referral in Pastoral Counseling*. Philadelphia: Fortress, 1969. A book written for pastors, with much that is applicable to lay counselors who need to refer their counselees.

REFERENCES

Arvidson, Marvin. 1977. A marriage and family counselor from Minneapolis. Adapted from a presentation at a couples' retreat at the Covenant Campground, Lake Geneva, Wisconsin.

Bassell, Ruth. n.d. Quoted in Richard O. Heilman, "Dynamics of Drug Dependency." Minneapolis: Alcohol and Drug Unit, Veterans Administration Hospital.

Blum, Eva Marie and Richard H. 1974. *Alcoholism: Modern Psychological Approaches to Treatment.* San Francisco: Jossey-Bass.

Brammer, Lawrence M. 1973. *The Helping Relationship: Process and Skills.* Englewood Cliffs, N.J.: Prentice-Hall.

Braun, Jay and Darwyn E. Kinder. 1979. *Psychology Today.* New York: Random House.

Brister, C. W. 1964. *Pastoral Care in the Church.* New York: Harper & Row.

Brunner, Emil. 1952. *Dogmatics.* Vol. 2. *The Christian Doctrine of Creation and Redemption.* Philadelphia: Westminster.

Brussel, James A., and Theodore Irwin. 1973. *Understanding and Overcoming Depression.* New York: Hawthorn.

Bustanoby, Andre. 1977. "Rapid Treatment for a Troubled Marriage," in Wright, *Training Christians to Counsel.* Denver: Christian Marriage Enrichment.

Butler, J. Donald. 1962. *Religious Education.* New York: Harper & Row.

Caplan, Gerald. 1964. *Principles of Preventive Psychiatry.* New York: Basic Books.

Chafin, Kenneth. 1966. *Help! I'm a Layman.* Waco: Word.

Clinebell, Howard J., Jr. 1979. *Growth Counseling.* Nashville: Abingdon.

___ and Charlotte H. Clinebell. 1970. *The Intimate Marriage.* New York: Harper & Row.

Collins, Gary. 1976. *How To Be a People Helper.* Santa Ana: Vision House.

___. 1972. *Effective Counseling.* Carol Stream, Ill.: Creation House.

___. 1972. *Fractured Personalities.* Carol Stream, Ill.: Table.

Combs, Arthur W., et al. 1971. *Helping Relationships: Basic Concepts for the Helping Professions.* Boston: Allyn and Bacon.

Conger, John J. 1977. *Adolescence and Youth.* 2nd ed. New York: Harper & Row.

Cosgrove, Mark P. and James D. Mallory, Jr. 1977. *Mental Health: A Christian Approach.* Grand Rapids: Zondervan.

Cousins, Norman. 1979. *Anatomy of an Illness.* New York: Norton.

Crabb, Lawrence J., Jr. 1977. *Effective Biblical Counseling.* Grand Rapids: Zondervan.

Drakeford, John W. 1961. *Counseling for Church Leaders.* Nashville: Broadman.

Eastwood, Cyril. 1963. *The Royal Priesthood of the Faithful.* London: Epworth.

Egan, Gerard. 1975. *The Skilled Helper.* Monterey, Calif.: Brooks/Cole.

Frankl, Viktor E. 1965. *The Doctor and the Soul.* trans. Richard Winston and Clara Winston, New York: Vintage.

___. 1975. *The Unconscious God.* New York: Simon and Schuster.

Glasser, William. 1965. *Reality Therapy.* New York: Harper & Row.

Goodell, John, Tom Kohout, and Joe Norquist. 1978. *The Butcher, the Baker, the Candlestick Maker.* St. Paul: St. John's Hospital.

Grimes, Howard. 1962. *The Rebirth of the Laity*. Nashville: Abingdon.

Grunlan, Stephen A., and Marvin K. Mayers. 1979. *Cultural Anthropology: A Christian Perspective*. Grand Rapids: Zondervan.

Harkness, Georgia. 1962. *The Church and Its Laity*. Nashville: Abingdon.

Hauch, Paul A. 1973. *Overcoming Depression*. Philadelphia: Westminster.

Heilman, Richard O. n.d. "Early Recognition of Alcoholism and Other Drug Dependencies," Minneapolis: Alcohol and Drug Unit, Veterans Hospital.

Henry, Carl F. H. 1980. "Evangelicals: Out of the Closet but Going Nowhere?" *Christianity Today*. 4 January.

Hoff, Lee Ann. 1978. *People in Crisis*. Reading, Mass.: Addison-Wesley.

Holmes, T. H. and R. H. Rahe. 1963. "The Holmes and Rahe Social Readjustment Rating Scale." *Journal of Psychometric Research*.

Howe, Reuel. 1952. *Man's Need and God's Action*. New York: Seabury.

———. 1959. *The Creative Years*. Greenwich: Seabury.

Hulme, William E. 1956. *Theology and Counseling*. Philadelphia: Muhlenberg.

———. 1970. *Pastoral Care Come of Age*. Nashville: Abingdon.

Hyder, O. Quentin. 1971. *The Christian's Handbook of Psychiatry*. Old Tappan, N.J.: Revell.

Jellinek, E. M. 1968. *The Disease Concept of Alcoholism*. New York: The College and University Press.

Johnson, Vernon E. 1973. *I'll Quit Tomorrow*. New York: Harper & Row.

Keil, C. F. 1949. *Biblical Commentary on the Old Testament: The Pentateuch*. 3 vols. Grand Rapids: Eerdmans.

Kelley, Robert K. 1969. *Courtship, Marriage and the*

Family. New York: Harcourt, Brace and World.

Kennedy, Eugene. 1977. *On Becoming a Counselor: A Basic Guide for Non-Professional Counselors.* New York: Seabury.

Kittel, Gerhard, ed. 1967. *Theological Dictionary of the New Testament.* 10 vols. Grand Rapids: Eerdmans.

Kline, Nathan S. 1974. *From Sad to Glad: Kline on Depression.* New York: Putman.

Koteskey, Ronald L. 1980. *Psychology from a Christian Perspective.* Nashville: Abingdon.

Kraemer, Hendrik. 1959. *A Theology of the Laity.* Philadelphia: Westminster.

Kubler-Ross, Elisabeth. 1969. *On Death and Dying.* New York: MacMillan.

Landorf, Joyce. 1974. *Mourning Song.* Old Tappan, N.J.: Revell.

Lasswell, Marcia, and T. E. Lasswell. 1982. *Marriage and the Family.* Lexington: Heath.

Lyons, Christopher A. 1973. "The Healing Ministry of the Holy Spirit." A sermon delivered at the Wheaton Bible Church, Wheaton, Ill., 23 September.

McCarthy, Raymond G., ed. 1964. *Alcohol Education for Classroom and Community.* New York: McGraw-Hill.

McLemore, Clinton M. 1974. *Clergyman's Psychological Handbook.* Grand Rapids: Eerdmans.

Mayers, Marvin K. 1974. *Christianity Confronts Culture.* Grand Rapids: Zondervan.

Minirth, Frank B. 1977. *Christian Psychiatry.* Old Tappan, N.J.: Revell.

___ and Paul D. Meier. 1978. *Happiness Is a Choice: A Manual on the Symptoms, Causes, and Cures of Depression.* Grand Rapids: Baker.

Nelson, Wesley W. 1979. "Depression Can Be Fatal," *Covenant Companion.* 1 October.

Nowlis, Helen J. 1969. *Drugs on the College Campus.* Garden City, N.Y.: Doubleday.

Oates, Wayne E. 1974. *Pastoral Counseling*. Philadelphia: Westminster.

——. 1953. *The Bible in Pastoral Care*. Philadelphia: Westminster.

Oglesby, William B., Jr. 1969. *Referral in Pastoral Counseling*. Philadelphia: Fortress.

Pelikan, Varoslav and Walter A. Mansen, eds. 1967. *Luther's Works*. St. Louis: Concordia Publishing House.

Pretzel, Paul W. 1972. *Understanding and Counseling the Suicidal Person*. Nashville: Abingdon.

Rogers, Carl R. 1961. *On Becoming a Person*. Boston: Houghton Mifflin.

Rogers, W. F. 1963. "The Pastor's Work with Grief," *Pastoral Psychology*. 14 September.

Schaeffer, Francis A. 1968. *The God Who Is There*. Downers Grove, Ill.: InterVarsity.

Shedd, Charlie W. 1971. *Is Your Family Turned On?* Waco: Word.

Slovic, Paul, Baruch Fishchoff, and Sarah Lichtenstein. 1980. "Risky Assumptions," *Psychology Today*. June.

Snyder, Howard. 1980. "Ministry Is for All Believers," *Covenant Companion*. 15 February.

Sobey, Francine. 1970. *The Nonprofessional Revolution in Mental Health*. New York: Columbia University Press.

Sperry, Len. 1978. *The Together Experience*. San Diego: Beta Books.

Stephens, William N. 1970. "Predictors of Marital Adjustment," in *A Marriage Reader*, Lloyd Saxton, ed. Belmont, Calif.: Wadsworth.

Stewart, Charles William. 1970. *The Minister as Marriage Counselor*. Rev. ed. Nashville: Abingdon.

Strong, James. 1980. *A Concise Dictionary of the Words in the Greek Testament*. New York: Abingdon-Cokesbury.

Sullender, R. Scott. 1980. "Three Theoretical Approaches to Grief." *The Journal of Pastoral Care.*

Taber's Cyclopedic Medical Dictionary. 1975. 12th ed. Philadelphia: F. A. Davis, Inc.

Thorn, George, ed. 1977. *Harrison's Principles of Internal Medicine.* 8th ed. New York: McGraw-Hill.

Ward, Waylon O. 1977. *The Bible in Counseling.* Chicago: Moody.

Welter, Paul. 1978. *How to Help a Friend.* Wheaton, Ill.: Tyndale.

Wright, H. Norman. 1977. *Training Christians to Counsel.* Denver: Christian Marriage Enrichment.